Fear of Dreaming

BOOKS BY JIM CARROLL

Living at the Movies
The Basketball Diaries
The Book of Nods
Forced Entries: The Downtown Diaries 1971–1973

RECORDINGS BY JIM CARROLL

Catholic Boy
Dry Dreams
I Write Your Name
Praying Mantis
A World Without Gravity:
   The Best of the Jim Carroll Band

Fear of Dreaming

the selected poems of

Jim Carroll

penguin  poets

PENGUIN BOOKS
Published by the Penguin Group
Penguin Books USA Inc., 375 Hudson Street, New York, New York 10014, U.S.A.
Penguin Books Ltd, 27 Wrights Lane, London W8 5TZ, England
Penguin Books Australia Ltd, Ringwood, Victoria, Australia
Penguin Books Canada Ltd, 10 Alcorn Avenue, Toronto, Ontario, Canada M4V 3B2
Penguin Books (N.Z.) Ltd, 182–190 Wairau Road, Auckland 10, New Zealand

Penguin Books Ltd, Registered Offices:
Harmondsworth, Middlesex, England

First published in Penguin Books 1993

10 9 8 7 6 5 4 3 2 1

Mr. Carroll's *Living at the Movies* (Grossman Publishers; Copyright © Jim Carroll, 1973) is reprinted in its entirety in this volume. Some of the poems in *Living at the Movies* previously appeared in the following publications: *Adventures in Poetry*, *Angel Hair*, *Another World* (Bobbs-Merrill), *Best & Co.*, *"C" Magazine*, *Chicago*, *The Chicago Seed*, *4 Ups & Down* (Angel Hair), *The New Poets* (Bantam), *Organic Trains* (Penny Press), *The Paris Review*, *Penumbra*, *Poetry*, *Reindeer*, *Stone Winds*, *Telephone*, *The World*, *The World Anthology*, and *The Young American Poets #2* (Follett). "Heroin" and "Silver Mirrors" were originally published in *The Yale Lit.* Copyright © The Yale Lit., 1969. Reprinted with permission.

Many of the selections from the author's *The Book of Nods* (Viking Penguin; Copyright © Jim Carroll, 1986) are reprinted in this collection. Some of these poems were first published in *Big Sky*, *Little Caesar*, *The Paris Review*, *Rolling Stone*, *The Transatlantic Review*, and *Walker Arts Center Broadside*. Others appeared on the records *Life Is a Killer* (Giorno Poetry systems) and *One World Poetry* (Dutch Imports from The World Poetry Festival, Amsterdam), in the film *Poetry in Motion* (director Ron Mann, Canadian Films), and in the video *The Cutting Edge* (M.T.V. and I.R.S. Records). Four poems have been added to the "New York City Variations" section; the selection on page 191 was first published in *The Paris Review*.

Among the poems in the section entitled "New Works 1989–1993," several of them appeared on the record *Praying Mantis* (Giant Records).

LIBRARY OF CONGRESS CATALOGING IN PUBLICATION DATA
Carroll, Jim.
Fear of dreaming : the selected poems of Jim Carroll / Jim Carroll.
p. cm.
ISBN 0 14 058.695 4
I. Title.
PS3553.A7644A6 1993
811'.54—dc20 93-1719

Printed in the United States of America
Set in Caslon 540

Special thanks to Susan Friedland,
Gerry Howard, and Paul Slovak.

Contents

Living at the Movies   *1*

Blue Poles   *3*
The Distances   *4*
The Narrows   *6*
August   7
Traffic   *8*
Styro   *9*
Morning   *10*
Next Door   *12*
The Green Bus   *13*
The Loft   *15*
In the Valley   *16*
The Burning of Bustin's Island   *17*
˙ Love Rockets   *18*
The Other Garden   *19*
Heroin   *21*
Poem   *23*
Birthday Poem   *24*

Seltzer   26
Living at the Movies   27
Your Daughter   29
Fragment: Little N.Y. Ode   30
Cough Syrup   31
One Flight Up   32
How Relaxed   33
For Ezra Pound   34
The Blue Pill   35
Blood Bridge   36
Poem on My Son's Birthday   37
Crossed Wires   38
Leaving N.Y.C.   39
A Fragment   40
Vacation   41
A Short Reminder   43
Gliding   45
To a Poetess   47
The Cosmopolitan Sense   50
Growing Up   52
Poem   53
Cold Faces   54
To the Secret Poets of Kansas   55
Jet Fizzle   56
Sea Battle   57
An Early Morning Crucifixion   58
Invisible Sleep   59
Sure . . .   61
Fear and Trembling   62
After St. John of the Cross   64

Little Ode on St. Anne's Day   *66*

Chop Chop   *67*

Silver Mirrors   *68*

Highway Report   *69*

Dog Crunch   *71*

Love Poem (Later)   *72*

California Poem   *73*

Withdrawal Letter   *74*

Maybe I'm Amazed   *76*

Mercury Clouds   *78*

New Year 1970   *79*

Midnight   *80*

Prell   *81*

Back Home   *82*

For Sue's Birthday   *83*

Song   *85*

Poem   *86*

Love Story   *87*

In This Room Particularly   *88*

The Tenth Try   *89*

Love Poem   *90*

For Your Birthday   *91*

Poem   *92*

On the Rush   *93*

Words from Babylon   *94*

Torn Canvas   *95*

The Birth and Death of the Sun   *96*

It Doesn't Matter   *97*

Chelsea May   *98*

Savage Bubbles   *99*

Paregoric Babies   *101*
An Apple at Dawn   *102*

The Book of Nods   *105*

Trained Monkey   *107*
With van Gogh   *108*
A Poet Dies   *110*
Homage to Gerard Manley Hopkins   *112*
Watching the Schoolyard   *117*
Guitar Voodoo   *118*
My Father's Vacation   *122*
Quality   *123*
Post Office   *124*
The Ice Capades   *126*
"The Academy of the Future Is Opening Its Doors . . ."   *127*
Parting the Reeds   *128*
The Lakes of Sligo   *129*
Lenses   *130*
A Beach Landing   *131*
Zeno's Final Paradox   *132*
Paraguay   *133*
The Safe Corridor   *134*
Rimbaud Scenes: *136*
    Rimbaud's Tooth Ache   136
    Rimbaud Sees the Dentist   137
    Waking in a Painter's Loft in Paris   138
    Rimbaud Running Guns   138
    Rimbaud Pays Homage to Saint Helena   140
Confederate Lake   *142*

One Hundred Years of Boredom   *143*
Silent Money   *144*
Scouting   *146*
Five Irresponsible Students of Zen   *147*
The Buddha Reveals Himself   *149*
Me, Myself, and I   *150*
Teeth Marks   *151*
Reaching France   *153*
In the Law Library   *154*
In the Capital   *155*
Stepping Out of M.O.M.A.   *156*
Days   *157*
The Transient   *164*
Just Visiting   *167*

New York City Variations   *171*

Poems 1973–1985   *195*

Poem   *197*
Winter's Age   *198*
For Elizabeth   *199*
Prologue   *201*
M. Verdoux, The Wife Killer   *202*
A Night Outing   *203*
Wing and Claw   *204*
The Ad Man's Daughter   *205*
Saint Theresa   *206*
In Four Seasons   *207*

Dead Salamander's Song   *208*
Painting by Flashlight   *209*
Heroes   *210*
Nightclubbing   *211*
Post-Modernism   *212*
The Caves   *213*
Judging the Pageant   *214*
El Hombre del Ombre   *215*
A Window in Cherry Valley   *216*
On Tour   *217*
Dueling the Monkey   *218*
A Child Growing Up with the Sun   *219*
For John Donne   *220*
Eugene, Oregon   *221*
Our Desires   *222*
My Debt   *223*
On Susan's Birthday   *224*
Poem   *225*
Dresden to Chesapeake Bay   *226*
In the Deep Green Vase   *227*
Poem   *228*
The New Death   *229*
The Runners   *231*
3 Short Poems: *232*
    Poem   232
    Compassion   232
    Cinco de Mayo   232
Things That Fly   *233*
For Robert Smithson   *234*
Borges Death Mask   *235*

The Desert Casino   236
Music Television   237
Sleeplessness   238
In the Gears   239

New Work 1 9 8 9 – 1 9 9 3   241

Curtis's Charm   243
A Perfect Stranger   255
I Am Not Kurt Schwitters   257
Calm Under Fire   259
Fear of Dreaming   260
Poem   261
Epiphany   262
Inauguration Day   264
In Time, AIDS   266
Song   267
Evening News   268
Praying Mantis   269
Micky   270
To the National Endowment for the Arts   271
Coda   273

About the Author   275

Living at the Movies

For Devereaux

Blue Poles

Blue poles (well?) on the beach
in a snowless winter and

I'm too cold to ask you
why we're here but of course "we are"

where on the puzzled reef dwarves either
fish or drown in the abandoned ships

sharks dissever year-old children in search
of "young blood" Jersey acting like Europe

in an instant and lovely Mary kneeling along the quick tide
to be anxious with thoughts of bare oceans

that move as the thighs of an eventual sunlight
like bathers moving closer to their season

when again gulls perch in their lovely confusion
"alone," as now, the sand sifting through

your fingers like another's darkness. it's true,
you are always too near and I am everything

that comes moaning free and wet
through the lips of our lovely grind

The Distances

The accumulation of reefs
piling up one over the others
like thoughts of the sky increasing as the head rises
unto horizons of wet December days perforated
with idle motions of gulls . . . and our feelings.

I've been wondering about what you mean,
standing in the spray of shadows before an ocean
abandoned for winter, silent as a barque of blond hair.

and the way the clouds are bending, the way they "react"
to your position, where your hands close over your breasts
like an eyelid approving the opening of "an evening's light."

parasites attach themselves to the moss covering
your feet, blind cubans tossing pearls across the jetty,
and the sound of blood fixes our eyes on the red waves.

                                    it is a shark!

and our love is that rusted bottle . . . pointing north,
the direction which we turn, conjuring up our silver knives
and spoons and erasing messages in the sand, where you wrote

"freezing in the arctic of our dreams," and I said
"yes" delaying the cold medium for a time
while you continued to "cultivate our possessions"

as the moon probably "continued" to cradle.
tan below the slant of all those wasted trees
while the scent carried us back to where we were:

dancing like the children of great diplomats
with our lean bodies draped in bedsheets and
leather flags while the orchestra made sounds
.

which we thought was the sky, but was only a series
of words, dying in the thick falsetto of mist.
for what can anyone create from all these things:

the fancied tilt of stars, sordid doves
burning in the hollow brick oven, oceans
which generalize tears. it is known to us

in immediate gestures, like candle drippings
on a silk floor. what are we going to do with anything?
besides pick it up gently and lay it on the breath

of still another morning. mornings which are
always remaining behind for one thing or another
shivering in our faces of pride and blooming attitude.

in the draught of winter air my horse is screaming
you are welcoming the new day with your hair leaning
against the sand. feet dive like otters in the frost

and the sudden blue seems to abandon as you leap. O
to make everything summer! soldiers move along lines
like wet motions in the violent shade's reappearance.

but what if your shadow no longer extends to my sleeping?
and your youth dissolves in my hand like a tongue, as
the squandered oceans and skies will dissolve into a single plane

(so I'll move along that plane)   unnoticed and gray
as a drift of skulls over the cool Atlantic where I am
standing now, defining you in perhaps, the only word I can.

as other words are appearing, so cunningly, on the lips
of the many strips of light. like naked bodies
stretched out along the only beach that remained,
brown and perfect below the descending of tides.

The Narrows

for Carol Kane

That is the way you are, always given
to silence. so I don't care anymore
about these green leaves in my carpet
about the death of an historical figure
about your voice.

you were thinking about a red curtain
that we might hide behind. I was
thinking about the freedom of your shadow,
last night, when this livid sky unfolded
its vault of a thousand swords and the air
we were breathing seemed our own.

I'm glad that you're able to breathe
I'm glad that you're able to distinguish me
from the lights along the thruway.
I mean don't both of us illuminate
the direction which you are taking?
and don't both weep nervously above
the moist pavement where you move.

I'd like to watch myself holding you
above the cool shore of something really vast
like a vast sea, or ocean.
and when I was through watching
I'd become someone else, seducing the heavy
waters, allowing nothing to change.
as the sands are changing and night comes
and we're not aware of all this endlessness,
which is springing up like The Moonlight Sonata
ascending from the glare of a thousand frightened moans.

August

The shower of black infants across the infected landscape . . .
birds, glaringly inhibited, as they dissolve
into the disappearance of boundaries
on a sea, filthy and darkened with bodies,
where passion rests beside the white canvas . . .

I'm lost again as I'm waking
as a wave would wake had it reached the shore:
it's like movement, something which bores us terribly,
but remains for a time to be never forgotten.

as somewhere there is a series of colors
winging their imperfect light
above your feeble reaction to it all
and spreading like blankets of trees in winter
onto the cold metal surrounding you.

while all I'm doing is gliding
toward some future, composed of plants and stones,
that passionate oasis, aware of fire dragged
through the mist of all those other possibilities:
moonlike emotion over this flat harbor,
moon exhausted across your embarrassed hand
where I finger this light eventually
of the rainbow you have constructed
like numbers along the map of some great thruway
thoughtlessly arranging some final confusion:

in the morning up early to look for you.

Traffic

I was a young pilot in World War I, remember?
do you know the feeling of an airplane crashing the water's edge?

we've just traveled 600 miles, and the only person
we know is sleeping under the wet almond tree.

there is nothing left but this meadow which smells of blood,
an infant has escaped from the orphanage long enough to be
    crushed
various birds admit their secret hate for us
and the canoe makes way through the cave for the abandoned
    North.

these fields open gently . . .
and the soft flowers are radiated within.

Styro

We'll stay until ice begins
over the driftwood

do you,
a girl from kansas,
imagine the invisible changes
in front of you?
and water wed constantly to sand
by foam beads . . .

pure directions of the sun
level the ocean
in your cupped palms

gulls play in their crude reflection
a tanker passes to split Europe

there is no other place that allows us
to understand so little, you see . . .

all those minds shot down by a cloud's emptiness

and our youth clung tightly
in white dunes . . .
they'll see us dreaming there
clumsy in these plaid blankets
at night.   it's

like watching wind push seaflowers
straight across your eyelids
or the sun melt them, either way

they'll be gone eventually
and new forms will take shape
and grow, even before we're gone

this will happen.

Morning

1.

Today the room is filled with tomorrows   the machines failed con-
tinuously   they got undressed   the tools being electric   three
elbows cast in light   the sculptor's dreams spilling like gray mar-
bles   one over the other shadow   speed fell along the wooden desk
downstairs the rape continued   a boy screaming for his cat   win-
dows crawled with vines   you are discovering your eyes carved in
enamel   over the dictionary flew last slabs of plaster   what is that
you needed from the clinic?

we could have afforded more than this   one does not pay for leaf,
sooty tear, membrane, or rare tints of ember   and receiving is acting
fatal, I guess   clocks alone maintained their retarded movement   or
darkness maybe   now I can think of her   lost in the fine spray of
a stream beside a dog's leg   you wanted so much more   hour hands
folding over like green sandwiches "this earth is slowly . . ."   a nail
tore apart the fruit later we moved upstate and lit fires on the
lawn   China provided lanterns   underwater the squid evidently
didn't reach the road   everybody joined us at the bar   it is a holyday
in France   a speaker remains on the stout platform.

2.

proper authorities served us with precautions   the light toppled the
aluminum support   "first the basement . . . then the border patrol"
but pretending one was another was a nauseous feeling   I want eyes
in your left arm   I'm not easy to please didn't I tell you?   rivers
are beginning to evaporate the chalk figures the children made   this
day seems destined to look like salt in the theater alcohol flew   from
the mezzanine   the final results came uptown   in the warehouse
the discussed inventory: a red garter belt   coffee   17 thighs   and
the tainted strainer   she incorporates the ideas   pearls are dipped
in August   everything was shuffled along the steaming tennis court
even the water had finished acting sly.

the other actresses ground flowers on the indian's skull   your breast a brick white and longer than the extremely cold bamboo   "I limit myself, yes," said the dog,   "but I'm happy,"   I seemingly can't take any suspense   all these abandoned slums   the sabres attached themselves to the gasoline foam   which was only a measuring stick which was only feet and yards   giving a geometry to our feelings in stepped the victim   out ran the prison walls freckled in some sections with brown ink.

the white chair suspended dignity   soon the impeccable aunt who came to visit   her mouth had been jammed with leather mechanically an oven boiling scotch tape   the dust opened to our hands like blue roses   fire engines avoided the yellow detour   "I must laugh if I tell you this, but I only feel like a torpedo now and then"   barb wire hawks surrounded the barn   12 year-olds peddled downhill right into the thorn berries   his ankle swollen by the pace "we won the pennant at last!"   later he returned in a bread truck all were dancing in the ochre garden   the negro maid put in the token   her husband praying like dice   the old cornices   clarinets were mistaken for red lightbulbs   there is never anything remaining for ransom money though, was there?   we always desire the excess: abundance of tri-colored petals   texture of the funneled wind   tinseled vapors dripped like feathers into the aquarium   our ring of meteors collapsed   soon the amusement park was destroyed   desire is clipped like angel hair   falling everything   even the dark green landscape   tree by tree   forest by forest.

Next Door

Today a hockey player died in
my dreams the lady takes her vows
I'm a nun the hallway is ringing with
drunks a cat sleeps on the roof
black as six years of snow that's
Tom my brother age one more than
me I'm 18 and you? you're lovely
thinking about my future the poems
laid waste in my head the stone
comes through the window like an
owl breaks everything into replace-
able parts like the poems laid waste
in my head the phone is trying to
tell us something my sky is a
friendly dome I'm so near to
everything yes H. Read making
coffee out of mold the kitchen
is burning basketballs "roll"
carrying all our energy of youth
warm gyms on wet Sundays the
pain of heat on concrete are you
trying to escape like evening?

A. Pope letting *his* amber fall
on *my* thorns O death of shepherd
me! O half-dressed shades of
voluptuous gold this whole night
while I love you as I watch you
where you are sleeping still perfectly warm

The Green Bus

What time is it in your bedroom?
the streets are becoming the red sea
            flushed through the white forest
where Gauguin was last seen saying goodbye

        despair in America (and Europe) oh!
we are here on 53rd and 6th watching steel
                        change to ivy   taxi's
sexy dreams pierce your left ventricle
                your left wrist is broken,

but the time!
            a wristwatch quickly sliding down the facade
it is 5 a.m.
        time to anticipate
            we anticipate
what we anticipate is a vision:
foresight among the fathers slowly withdrawing from the legion
seeking the insoluble answer of the waves   I mean the streets
do you realize "I hate you"   now you sneeze

(it isn't easy talking to you
            through the brick genitals you're holding,
and I tremble without boots or wings,
sitting exhausted upon the serpent's breath

a fan moves in the sky   you are a very happy person
it drips the sordid blood
                it stops . . .   the heat!
        it is 5 a.m. in the Warwick Coffee Shop
it is 5:10 in N.Y.
                    I am in N.Y. . . .

"no more fiesta along Houston St." she remarked
        "smear the river with doves and praise
                        the departing feathers"

■

13

(I don't know from your bedroom what you're thinking,
        said the "person"   do you want to take in a movie,
and go home after and fuck maybe?

                you are warm today and the climate
                                is happy and welcomed

shall we walk, then, to the park?
            near the fountain?
                        shall we sit in the grass?

14

The Loft

So I move through the black doorway
to be turned headon into light
and the phone was desperate
to speak to tell you something
in the next room she pants like 8th St.
the drawers swept the powdery substance
through the green shaft and
it was Thursday because of your breath.

(the effulgence of your sway
and total landscape of clockblood

I have produced the ransom once more
and the third of five angels is set free
to resurrect / and be buried again

so that I hardly remember the
composed landscape and waters
the rose violin the basketball teams

I was happy as you were about the whole thing
I saved for months . . . the calendar is crushed
"put on your rifle," they told her, "death
is only white by nature"
evening is so vain lately
like your lips geometry.

should anything have come to this, love?
take the yellow typewriter,
it's winter   I'm so glad
and the wind is pushing like pinecones
against the angel's dying sperm.

In the Valley

Everyone's eyes broke
when they woke earlier than usual
today
to the hum of the winter moth

mostly we fixed windows after that
it was worse than when we tried
to make the ceiling flat
again
after the heavy rains last Spring

after rainy lunch at the fountain
we assembled ladders and attacked
the snowbirds that gather along the wires
when the sun's half cut by the mountain.

flowers, eagles and children
twice the size of other children,
demagnetizing skybulbs,
the factory . . . and retired celebs
are what we are proudest of here . . .

Tonight we play with needles
in our ponchos, wavering,
it is cool, it is clear . . .
it is wholesome in this valley

The Burning of Bustin's Island

As you enter the room a door knob
possibly hundreds of years older than your oldest relative . . .

work has suddenly offered its hand to me like a boxer
and noises round and for the most part fake have crept . . .

on the lawn a green bike leans its broken fender
against the pinecone, a boy waves then throws the ball into . . .

light producing a condition between which nothing
grows and horses spring up like a field must . . .

sooner or later a bench near the eastern cove will
dump its clients overboard and they will have mud . . .

at last a breath of fresh sea water, spray reoccurring
like a day a dream close to the shadow of speed . . .

split by light and dark.

Love Rockets

Wet leaves along the threshold of the mid-day
and I'm off to rescue the sky from its assassins
jogging and screaming and launching my clean mortars

into the March obscene air . . . the enemy.

I suppose I'd rather be sitting in Samoa now
sipping a quart of Orange Julius and being fanned
by Joey Heatherton in black tights and white glossy lipstick.
but I'm not. I'm here. and I have something to say,

as well as something to take care of.

And that something is probably more important than
you realize. I like the sky (don't you) its warmth, its friendliness,
I'm not going to let all this fucking soot taint that terrific blue.

battle the filthy airs with your mortars and your prayers.

you'll soon be overcome with lovely sensations of the sky.
you'll be thinking of me as this happens.

The Other Garden

Now I want to return
for your fingers are like a thousand silk ponies
mounted along the icy miles.
    "the exquisite grasp of this land we do love
                and awake to on Sundays"
but what is time since you've discovered what it means?
we are dying now like frozen breath,
and our hands are extended far out into the hordes of light.

now I want to return because we were
always there anyway weren't we
when the telephone wire stretched
across the farther valley, supporting
the tiny snow birds, the day the ranger
arrived and presented us desire. the shallow
rocks swallowing the frog, three of us
pulling our fingers away from the frightened moss
"home" you might have called it,
it was evening continuously, or at least not morning
the winds of lice sweeping us over some future nation
(I wasn't built by any process other than
                the poem itself, thus I am ashamed
                of making distinctions like this.)
distance falling over the wet colors
like mauve tongues, the fowl was taken
behind the barn . . . last week . . . your eyes
are like squashed hands . . . I can't stand it . . .
it's snowing green handbags . . . I'm falling . . . dark reeds
are lost upon the lips . . . I adore you.
now I've lost the key again. through the window
came the split morning glories, as if
they knew about legs. there were so many more
incidents which you never really explained:
of the field, the magnet tugging at the appliance,
the grapefruit smile and of course
                the bed of sperm.

∎

but I never let myself be taken in
by that deep, flowing what? for I always
remembered you that way, like a clock
leaning on a breast; like a mouse.

Heroin

Sat for three days in a white room
a tiny truck of white flowers
was driving through the empty window
to warn off your neighbors
and their miniature flashlights.

by afternoon
across the lake
a blind sportsman had lost his canoe.
he swam
by evening
toward the paper cup
of my hand.

At dawn,
clever housewives tow my Dutch kitchen
across the lawn.
and in the mail a tiny circus
filled with ponies
had arrived.

You,
a woman with feathers
have come so often lately
under my rubber veranda
that I'm tearing apart all those tactless warnings
embroidered across your forehead.

Marc,
I'm beginning to see those sounds
that I never even thought
I would hear.

Over there a door is knocking
for example
with someone you hate.

and here I beg another to possess somehow
the warmth of these wooden eyes

so beside me
a lightbulb is revolving
wall to wall,
a reminder of the great sun
which had otherwise completely collapsed
down to the sore toe of the white universe.

its chalky light
rings
like a garden of tiny vegetables
to gather the quiet of these wet feelings
together

once again

like the sound of a watch
on your cold white wrist
which is reaching for a particular moment
to reoccur . . .

which is here . . . now.

Poem

We are very much a part of the boredom
of early Spring of planning the days shopping
of riding down Fifth on a bus terrified by easter.

but here we are anyway, surviving like a wet street in August
and keeping our eye on each other as we "do it," well,
you go west on 8th St. and buy something mystical to wear
and I'll simply tuck my hands into my corduroy pockets
and whistle over to Carter's for the poster he promised me.

I like the idea of leaving you for a while
knowing I'll see you again while boring books
W. H. Auden, and movie schedules sustain my isolation
and all the while my mind's leaning on you like my body
would like to lean on you below some statue in Central Park
in the lion house at the Bronx Zoo on a bed in Forest Hills on a
    bus.

I reach 3rd avenue, its blue traffic, I knew I would sooner
or later and there you are in the wind of Astor Place reading
a book and breathing in the air every few seconds
                                    you're so consistent.

Isn't the day so confetti-like? pieces of warm flesh tickling
my face on St. Mark's Place and my heart pounding like a negro
                                                        youth
while depth is approaching everywhere in the sky and in your
    touch.

Birthday Poem

1.
3 hours into the afternoon of March 9th
and the morning is still lingering like a cloud
reflected onto a building on 53rd St.
where I am.
the streets are much too involved   (with what?)
much too wet too   (with rain)
though I don't mind the rain
only the wet streets and
Ron Padgett might or might not agree with that,
but we're having breakfast together nonetheless.

2.
Ron Padgett is holding two birthday gifts
which come in the form of two books
one being the works of an Italian poet
whose name I quite honestly don't remember
the other book is some selected works of Zeno
whose thoughts on motion I find very entertaining
though they're not very useful   (for me at least)
the person about to receive these gifts
is George Schneeman, who is lucky enough
to be having a birthday today.
it's also lucky for Ron that this is true
because wouldn't it be embarrassing
giving George gifts today
if his birthday were, say, a week ago
or a week ahead.

3.
but everything has worked out fine,
not like the weather
which is as dark as a laundry closet
in a very "cheap" hotel
"on a day like this I feel like I'm indoors,"
says Ron walking
to the subway of France (?) well

it seems like France
for a time boarding the first car
and watching teenagers giving up
their seats to pregnant women
or those mutilated in the war and
anyone wearing one of those
tiny red pins   (get up Ron)

4.
it's still gray and wet almost pink
as we reach E. 14th and shake hands goodbye
like someone else I'm reminded of now
writing this poem.
and I catch the bus to Ted Berrigan's
who never showed up anywhere,
least of all here on E. 14th St.
right below Larry Rivers' studio
which is the route my bus is taking.

5.
I hope that George enjoys the gifts
that Ron will give him tonight.
I guess if I saw George now I'd
like to be holding something really valuable
to give him also.
but as things go (on E. 2nd St.) all I'm
holding is a 25¢ orange drink
and what would George Schneeman want that for
well I was thinking of something more valuable anyway,
like a Mercedes Benz or a great feeling
like I have right now,
just realizing that someone you know was born today.

Seltzer

1.
Here is my room, smiling like a forest
of navels   yet, in secret,
                        so sad and filthy.

2.
breathe deep enough and we are possessed.
breathe again and we will be gone.

3.
the best thing about today
is the idea of tomorrow.
                        we will go on a picnic.

4.
who can argue with 6000 swallows
flying from a single cloud,
                        like joy.

5.
when we die we might see the Virgin Mary
sitting before the father, the son, and the Holy Ghost

right now I'll settle for you
with your bra unhooked   (under a tree)
on the Staten Island ferry.

Living at the Movies
for Ted Berrigan

1.
There is a stadium beside my window
            filled with winter
and it is afternoon   alight and barrowing my tears
so by day the message arrives   and by night
I am writing.   marvelous joy of "being sure"
pain sweats the hunger upon its teeth   the days
of white miracles break through   sun over the Harlem River
2:23   the fields are gone, moist and trembling.
she plumbs to the purple earth
           light rising into her features.

2.
So months of cool flowers close in these arms:
decay with their green obscenity.   denial of everything
in an instant!
      (how strange to be gone)   (to be sure)
like René Magritte devouring an apple
                (or two)
that's my language,   divisions of words I know:
             "love:sky"

3.
It is afternoon   a sailor is crying above the waterfall
so we bend our heads and pretend to be praying   yes,
I have abandoned the starlets and their mothers
          and trees are growing on your avenue,
teeth sweating the hungry pain   takes her away in the form
of death or love and
      O to ease the stupidity of my dreams
in the orange wet of loneliness at midnight
           where in abandoned towers
a young shepherd is sleeping
(and you know it)

4.

Into a swamp this heart is flying
like Mayakovsky's last breath
      death full of gravity and Frank O'Hara
I have abandoned . . . and I am crying   it is midnight
and she knows it. marvelous joy of miracles breaks through
I lick the sweat upon the hungry pain.
I wonder if she's ever hungry
            I wonder if she's thinking of pain
it is midnight   she plumbs to the purple day
and O to think of her that way.

5.

light rising into her features where
into a swamp this poem is flying the
starlets and their mothers are gone
                  they plumb to the earth extinct
so all that's left is she   taken away in the form
                              of death or love.
the blue day breaks through in miracles.
the miracles are gone.   (how strange to be gone)
like Mayakovsky's last breath.   René Magritte
devouring the earth's plumb   light rising into
our features the dark obscenity and O to think
of her that way   it is morning and she is crying
the trees on her avenue are flying   wet orange loneliness
of her stupid dreams disappearing
            into a swamp where rise these purple days.

Your Daughter

In this month arks
deposit supplies along the shore

sand drenched . . .

     the river   suddenly the sea

now lifted up beside your heels
which warns of light in the eye of what you are holding.

your passion:

     a white mountain disappearing in the mirror.

to awake to the joy of your cold abstraction . . .
as horses returning somewhere her tight grasping the sea and air.

Fragment: Little N.Y. Ode

I sleep on a tar roof

     scream my songs
         into lazy floods of stars . . .

a white powder paddles through blood and heart

                  and

the sounds return

        pure and easy . . .

this city is on my side

Cough Syrup

There's a hockey puck in front of the air on the window sill

I see this contraption as infinity . . .

though it's covered with dust . . .
I want to touch it

but I'll have to wash my hands
because I got leukemia in N.Y. this afternoon

One Flight Up

The people upstairs are cold
the girl with the full-sized German shepherd
and the boy who sleeps with her
are rapping against the radiator
with a spoon, it sounds like.

their message must carry down
one more flight to the janitor
whose business this is.

I can hear the steam
already beginning
in the pipe beside me

and soon the pressure will carry it higher
and the entire building will be warmer,
thanks to them, to sleep in.

How Relaxed

The way a man sits
all day on a manhole cover
contemplating a rubber stamp,

until a volkswagen brushes by
on your arm
and you're left with an idea
of, say, a man washing windows

who would rather be teeing off
somewhere in Rye, N.Y.

green

For Ezra Pound

I watched the secret
head of Mussolini
bobbing like a wet balloon
behind a strolling bush
in Vermont's sticky dawn

I made a fist . . . but dig:

a healthy cricket sat
and noticed this too
and he immediately ex-
pelled a harmless goo

                        over the thought

of Mussolini (I swear)
running from me
to avoid getting snagged
and punished for his million atrocities.

The Blue Pill

I took the blue pill this morning

I got new angles on the trees across the driveway

Timmie the bear
does his little roll on the rug

and at night
a sound gathers the tiny ambulances
from their homes

it is distant and hollow

a little like the sound
of a perfectly tuned ocarina

Blood Bridge

White ship disappears
into wave machine . . . this morning

your eyes got shot with
secret chains

that pill armies eventually
set free.

you queens so often, in fact,
open my graceful anxieties

like soft horses through toy deserts . . .

I love this mansion
though it's too many windows

to open halfway each morning
to close halfway each night

Poem on My Son's Birthday

At dawn
on the window sill
it's watery trees it's light
it's just hanging there waiting

poetry

I want to walk   you can come or
you can sleep or
you can dream of walking someplace better

and that still means we're not together

      except today
      one more day   (you were born)

It's a communion
you can hardly see
a kind of reunion   just a little one

you and me.

Crossed Wires

In 1943 the Germans sent me postcards.

I laughed heartily.

now each new day heats my cavity
I hear light scratches in the walls
drink orange pekoe tea
and weep.

I've learned nothing
I've just watched children hang across the back yard
like glittering crossed wires
exposed with silver air.

Leaving N.Y.C.

I spent a wonderful day
with two real Dutch ladies
in postcard outfits
in front of a pleasant house
with a brown tiled roof
and a brick facade with blue windows
not thinking about poetry, music,
movies, paintings, priests or nuns,

or you.

A Fragment

When I see a rabbit
crushed by a moving van
I have dreams of maniac computers
miscalculating serious items
pertinent to our lives.

Vacation

White leaf trailing the water light

and of course the stones are too much for these waters
so if one sinks
colors fall upward and blind us.
you are surrounding "the edge" now
stockings shake some craggy wetness into my ear
where I hear strange sounds.

I guess it is too often:
your fingers slipping unto my eye
high in those mountains
like a hunter.
birds thrown upward
like a hand near a lake
and your face is held before the sun
as a letter attached to a tree.

that you
yellow as the June feathered air
should hike to my window this morning
and deliver this shape
like a heart lost
within a field no one can locate.
a calf's heart probably.

I don't know about meadows
once I rode a sled
through an entire month of summer
and never landed anywhere
bees touched me and went away
I was grateful for that but now
a tree has landed across my skinny chest.

the most complex dream
ends near a swamp . . .
and horses move inverted on the gas station ceiling

I would drop like a cocoon from space
but I don't understand the very atmosphere.
my legs curl in the fog.

now you are lying on your back letting
birds open your thighs and
like a gesture I fling these loose eyes
into the steam of August.
bricks dissolve around the riverbank.

it is what keeps me from you.

A Short Reminder

They've tricked you, these boundaries
the way each stares back to the next
hoping the change might occur.

but the organ started up again
as the hand tightened the grip
on the knob of the door
the way you only guessed it should be.

up until now the way a star
greets you so openly, you forgot
for a moment that it meant nothing afterall
thought tonight it was all you had ever hoped.

                              and you were right.

because the people are all gathered
along the cliffs . . . hung like breath
their hearts are like the pets
of some terribly dreary penthouse
as clouds descend to protect their dreams

then the trees pointed off . . . over there
where the man stands hunched over the slope
who was he? and what did he want?
becoming a part of it? that same "it"?
only more useless now, intricate as a nipple,
though so easily realized even along
the busiest streets of daylight, the spirit
that leaves you tangled in some later hour

                              which is here

where the paintings drop to the floor in rows
because you do not care to think about them again
now that you have developed this power to forget about pain
innocent, of course, but hands shaking nonetheless

you sit down in a restaurant and a glass
breaks on the heel of your shoe . . . people turn . . .
outside the window a pathway of heat guided from star to tree
breathless at first . . . but where is the solution?
and why the tree so alike each of the others, so that

when space comes into the formula the only thing
you concede is that you're "in it"

                                        guided by another like you

Gliding

Devereaux wakes this morning with a dream of mountains

  wind child with perfect breasts

      glides lightly

in sheer robes   white teeth

      her warm pets her

   wisdom plants

  I just have to move on

       in floppy hats

  70 m.p.h.

      cruising turnpikes for

  sun bubbles . . .

       pop open in mist

amazing grace

    up from cracked pavements

  more

    young girls in empty blouses

("You see through . . ." they

   squat against fire

      hydrants

with cupped hands inventing

        secrets that

               later you can't deny

   I watch

          little Jupiters whiz around my fingers

the space available to me

           from the place I sit

    to the place I dream

To a Poetess

You sit to have waves rush to your open hands
and you're surprised as cities grow there

     the cool air's
          driving flips

               jammed with mini-spearguns

but this time they're real
facing you,
        with your private school stripes

Miss Hewitt's girls riding through the reservoir
                        (on horse(s)

                the horizon goes limp
                  and finally
you're not so beautiful afterall

        . . .

my arms shoot stiff   I justify a margin

     in that sense
     each vein glows

        . . .

good   but what I really need

    a soft chair

      to nod on your boring rap
      I'd settle for a twelve year nap.

        . . .

you go on then:
I'll listen

     why either worry or hate or be confused . . .
    because the sun's so available and

mostly for you

bikini doll

      I quit listening again   I even go

with one tiny spit   on your black lace toe

■ ■ ■

It's better here
with the polar bears   good

better   so   light dissolves and swells my blood
                  a process worth remembering

    instead   (it's noon)   I watch solar colors
                  wash themselves on her skin

and She has nothing to do with you

■ ■ ■

six dozen wet beach umbrellas
the space between them

     fading and then dissolving America into "families":

I
don't
understand
any
of
this.

■ ■ ■

though You're worse than ever
better just make a date with never

48

                    with your bunches of radar fingers
you might as well dissever

                                        (giant aspirins
                                        in the sky)

relaxing the locked planets of this galaxy.

The Cosmopolitan Sense

An odyssey of error humbles the cosmopolitan
sense, Han's recurring heartache, his skipole
knifing a snowy bank on your pain,
and everything opens up like a racehorse
in a forest, something grows and the sidewalk lets go,
so faces move in from the rain throwing tools
and knives and questions, which, unanswered
close the covers of a book we insist on living in,
only there are roofs rising off the sidewalk
and small birds grab them in their beaks
to string them, these pearls, like beads or arrows
along the street that runs from here to Ferdinand's,
you know, the egoist with the split tongue.
To get there isn't easy under the roofs
fitted with dusty attics, perfect hideouts for books by moonlight
and tea by noon. Anything to clear the streets
of all those walkers, in fact anything to put near your ear
and cough by, anything to put in your pipe and smoke.
You see it doesn't matter if the rug comes out from under us,
because summer feels better in the desert in spite of the insects

who wish to nip our ears, but they are stopped
by a deadly spray under one roof, the spray of the sea,
as it rises to quench my thirst and it does
because I am innocent about death
and never wish to kill the idea
of a home, of a sad lonely night
when fiery ovals parachute out of the sky
picking up our heads so quickly the pipe
drops out of our mouth, and I reach to defend myself
knowing that forever I must stop the pain, the only purpose we're
    sure of
The rug comes out from under us
revealing fiery skies that think for themselves,
midnights overloaded with print, noon of the winds
knocking your window out over a bed, familiar as home
and the girder chained day, but you don't object

because it is the way of things to move in circles
partly because of color partly because of the great mountains
and trees thrown into it, like a pearl tossed
into a pod, the way some tiny gardener gets a thrill one day,
opening it up and becoming rich, thus a shiny new tractor
arrives and everyone sits down to watch.
We're all tiny gardeners in a sense, waiting for that tractor
and rehearsing without any clothes on as we move around and
    hope.
We're all things moved by color through mountains and into trees
thrilled by tiny gestures, a bright necktie, friendship, everything
tossing us: a frenzy, a blue, a giddy gulp.

written with Bruce Wolmer
& Charles Goldman

Growing Up

for George Schneeman

we got lucky not too long ago
you showed up &
we improved
& we improved you too & that's true
but not too much
you've got the silver
and we've got the change
which proves something you tell us
that bodies have some interest
like feathers & trees and air too
and we agree with this
we think it's true
& we know you and we are better for it
so ante up George
the tension is incredible,
                              mounting

written with Ted Berrigan & Bill Berkson

52

Poem

The tea is boiling
sun in morning shade

my eyes squint on a red sofa
my teeth brushed electrically in the bath room
the rest of me does yoga on the lawn

your wife is turning pale, she is sick
of the hindu next door, sparkling lice
nest in her hair . . . I see

water flowers shoot up on thin layers of ocean fog

your son is in the corner tossing an epileptic fit . . .

we start to feel enclosed
like mannequins in storage start
to shiver, figure out someway to occupy our minds

start to knit or something

Cold Faces

1.
you breathe
through your mouth

saturate all things
on this resort beach

2.
the lightning moves closer
up the stairway
I watch the storm

To the Secret Poets of Kansas

Just because I can't understand you
it doesn't mean I hate you . . . like
when you go on continuously how you
cannot tolerate skyscrapers or cabdrivers

                          maniac faces on Fifth, well

it means nothing to me I
just ignore as so often
or shift gears and read Pope or some
boring Russian lunatic . . . you can't deny future

                                 or simply fade.

and if you don't feel like running across streets here
you simply get run over and that means pain and boredom . . .
now isn't it amazing how you bring out logic in my poems.

I see nothing in a tree but lazy shade and nature
and that's not special, that's science

and all this concrete and steel and noise,
well, they've divided the simplest air to poems
some mornings, and we can't always rely on "Beauty" or gods

                                 you must learn

but so often on our losses . . . and our tears.

Jet Fizzle

It was summer then
and the forests were legal

the farmers there
use marble eggs as decoys

when those Hawks dive
they reach speeds up to 200 m.p.h.

disappointed

at egg

a switchman
a red lantern
in Grand Central Station

a jar of honey
in the plain brown bag

I thought
that it was pretty
weird

when he poured it in

God the fathers beard

Sea Battle

I fall out
crush the useless excess of god

my mouth most dry

each actor celebrates
his imminent "He must die"
shortage of great

like a chorus of nuns
every school morning . . . sing:

"child sang and child fell
and child rode right thru his shell
white plastic fish dissolve in that sea
I thank god for what has given me . . ."

SPECIAL WAVES
the sign reads

too many to see

the words say
"I be free,"
(I told her meant)
to change all eternity

so man lifts his head
forms his song
the land changes

as he murmurs

"It is as I said"

a president
or two

now and then found dead.

An Early Morning Crucifixion

Sands darkened by insects
and lights to measure the foggy distance,
we are going out there . . .   tonight
our pockets filled with the pressed blossom

                              across the giggling surf.

you had come here in secret and returned
and I barely saw the image against the warm grass,
it was more like a doctor or a soldier, because
to accept this breeze is to continue to choose, to distinguish.

                              you'll be quiet as that happens.

to see shadows on waves and the passion
tumble to the shore from this perfect edge,
to know the warmth of a hand placed diagonal
to the tree which a few minutes ago disappeared,

into a region where the cool stallion
tramples the night bather's wrist, and she
cries as if to warn the others to embrace,
bronze ladies running drenched along the gravel shores

Invisible Sleep
for Devereaux

Traces of pink Bergdorf light
dissolving into its furry air

nervously towed up
wrecked sidewalks

N.Y.C.'s bubble dawns
reminding me each year
of each year reversed

hazy puffed up sensibilities

                                            I stole somewhere

shoot out . . .

snow trips snow
its clumsy grey fingers
like insects rolling somewhere beneath you

                               invisible sleep of winter

Hotel Plaza's elegant
stare through abandoned nostalgia zoos
                         phantom playgrounds
                         chained noise trucks
dragging down Fifth

just reflectingly plain and wet there.

music manages itself as usual everywhere
and I get lost lately if there's no packages to carry

lame fountains tempt lame birds
school girls fill buses to return someplace dreaming
▪

and in the same room later on
I've been spacing my time
more often these days

                              the tiny notes of steam
releasing me, another year
in your thought out gaze.

Sure . . .

I got
a syringe

I use it
to baste
my tiny turkey

Fear and Trembling

To play Segovia
upon waking
is the highest I
might ever aspire to might
even shoot down the pain
dreams these hands
shake colorless they
can't forget and
in that way just can't defend

                              sun stirred
                                  in coffee
                                      by condensed air spoons

              and

on the bathroom floor on the porcelain there

                                  blue blood

from the terrace the reservoir
evaporates in the violet tubes of
morning air, chokes miniature landscapes . . .
none of these processes fail me

                          only the flower

              too distant to imagine even . . .

though you sleep through . . .

          sunken eyes   radiate the bed

                              empties the frost
                                  from the bars and windows

pouting torn   bending image
■

                    I watch the children you breathe dissolve
                    I see the plain girl the plain print gown

          then I figured out what was real
                                        blue blood

remember?   I noticed the morning and its sound

          I noticed the scar
          on your wrist as
          the palms rise
                              to catch each tear

After St. John of the Cross

We humans
do not freeze often

but rather the dragon breathes
and our wrists are jolted from the fogs,

Sun, speak to me,
you are important.

no, that's not fire,
that's reason   which you might enjoy

                             like a raisin

if the kitchen hadn't diminished
       before the trucks had arrived.

Mr. Hoffer,
       you are an enigma   I've decided
and earth
       you have flunked.

I am not impressed
by a cartoon character
who drives his hammer
against my thumb,

yet I goof
         on "a profound idea"

as I nod   in this century

     it squats in my hand   and licks,

folks,
      that isn't just any whistle
      that you happen to be hearing

•

it is a signal   it is 5 p.m.

now fold the ladder and
                    lay down the machete.

now run back through the rice paddy.

Little Ode on St. Anne's Day

You're growing up
and rain sort of remains
on the branches of a tree
that will someday rule the earth.

and that's good
that there's rain
it clears the month
of your sorry rainbow expressions

and clears the streets
of the silent armies . . .

so we can dance

Chop Chop

My pet creations fly away
I swat at pig air in the humid forest

I don't care for no bullshit, Mr. President,
I want thick quick cheeseburger

                        chop chop

you merchants have no idea how great
it is to be here   (right here)

flipping bubblerings around the little girls
and jotting down their names on stones

                        in the water

Prince, I hear the bed squeaking in the palace
because you and foxey are up to naughty naughty

it's great however
it's like being next to baby's breath

poor Spinoza!

he got excommunicated
because of some cosmic whim

and no one was allowed
within four cubits of him

Silver Mirrors

A horse moves
this weekend
into our living room

he says, "Oh, quickly
form a ring around me
as to prevent the merciless
insane hounds from attacking
my weakened legs in attempt
to drag me back to the icy
palace in the wintry regions."

"Then you are the one they sent?"

"yes"

"Very clever, did you bring it?"

"yes"

Highway Report

for Jack Kerouac

Breathe . . .
open fields
like tipping your hat to the sun

stream across turnpike

                    two women

on the other side   their dawns
reflect through the waters
on horses   tall weeds sensuous sway

crows settle

they assort their dreams

                              highway metal fences shine

three of us
feminine   marvelous   and tough

          our long hair
          rests on a cloud's eye
                              streaming

drinking codeine   and my body
at 70 m.p.h.   is feather

I raise a knife to the sky's neck
the sun curves to avoid me

(It didn't really curve)
the sun couldn't care less

                good afternoon,
                Mayakovsky
                          my nod:
                          a walk down St. Mark's Pl.

with Ray Bremser

wearing a kimono . . .

Here comes the sun
over a.m. radio

nodded two hours

nation's capital ascends over
trees colored for my dream
along yr. highway life

Kerouac is dead at 47

on radio

and McCartney alive

(we lost)   and

tragedy's just that and what to do but keep on going all in one line

■ ■ ■

the joggers are jogging
a president is lying

(Last month my prick was "discharging")

let us pray

Last highway trees and barns sway, the roads
sighing wetly . . . clouds so low, they are filled
with the snow of my heart, it's part of every man's
dream to rise to the sky . . . to die, gone forever from
American highways, where I nod today, missing nothing
really . . . to disappear . . . at least for a time

this clear October day.

Dog Crunch

The foot of
a dog
formed and crunched
a lake

as my ear
falls now

Love Poem (Later)
for Rise

The little bonus
of my hand on your breast
makes a bus seem so useful
when some rain begins to open.

then cloud waves cracked sun shafts
when the sky began to whistle
and I was thinking about it all night
just watching it move from my eye to my hand.

it's not very meaningless
the changes one makes lying down
it's almost the way a mountain feels
when it becomes a star

California Poem

The ocean fooled me
I thought it was bubble
but it was frozen spray
like a pain dream
and the double driftwood
and agates
surfers in rubber masks
and suits . . . like leather angels
leaning forward on their knees on
moon struck docks along Tenth Ave.
N.Y. . . . city of cowboy fantasies

and my own dreams beneath this blonde sun
of heroin and poolrooms childhood back home

you'll never return
yet you will go back
drawing more distinctions . . .
there, where my entire history
waits in sun puddles on filthy sidewalks
thousands of umbrellas poking my body

to wound the heart

and out here poets sleep beaches all day
with fears of Japan where bronze children
start landslides on their brains

Withdrawal Letter

Wild geese waking in the March wind

it's morning
I don't think much about March
though the weather disturbs me
and
the geese, they disappear eventually
with enormous groans of lost possibilities

I am truly a fragment of your secret worlds
though this eludes me. I think
all day about the likeness of heroin
to skindiving, how sharks never sleep
are marked from Southampton to Japan in three days

and how pure the waves are
no matter what the professors say,
in their motion . . . a gull glows in my sweat

                                                            Eastward

simple, yet the pain of remembering
so much before, so many gulls
seen and jammed into poems
this one just glided onto the reef
it was easy to include, and I trust it.

and horses, count the horses
in this poem and that
I saw a palomino once in Kansas and wept
the eye ring froze from each touch,
truck drivers passing on the highway
shouting with their fingers

though I nodded mostly through Kansas
treating someone I love badly, though
confusion results, and from there one realizes

74

it is not alone, anything
in the end, and one loves again
in this marvelous hollow decoration
each moves slowly within

you want to whisper, mainly of fear,
"Who are they?"

it is daylight now

the truth is you lost your willow
for me to find, for each muse to dance
why not joy to change pace
under these weeping leaves, only nature's gimmick

and "They," well, they surround you in N.Y.C.
on subways and park entrances near the plaza
but can you turn your head to the fountain?
I sit with my long hair breathing spray

and can I bear all those other scenes
so many other words might shoot up?

I want my hands and neck to be free and clear
no crucifixes and no rings.

these hands that hold the blood that rises
to a level where joy is pumped
visually to one's heart
in the serpent red dawn

Maybe I'm Amazed

Just because there is music
piped into the most false of revolutions

it cannot clean these senses
of slow wireless death crawling
from a slick mirror
1/8th its normal size . . .

Marty was found dead by the man literally
blue 12 hours after falling out
at the foot of the Cloisters
with its millions in rare tapestry
and its clear view of the Hudson

and even testing your blue pills
over and over to reverse
my slow situations
I wind up stretched across the couch
still nodding with Sherlock Holmes
examining our crushed veins

Richard Brautigan,
I don't care who you are fucking
in your clean california air

I just don't care

though mine are more beautiful anyway
        (though more complex perhaps)

and we have white flowers too
right over our window on 10th St.
like hands that mark tiny x's
across infinity day by day

but even this crumb of life
I eventually surface toward

continues to nod as if I see you all
thoughtlessly
through a carefully inverted piece
of tainted glass

shattered in heaven
and found on these streets

Mercury Clouds

The waves pumping at you

                        like mercury clouds

      just a section of the universe showing off

closer than you imagine
sea birds are planning

            to divide a revolution

closer than that a mother
feeding her baby

               (bright plaid beach chairs)

milk from the earth

        my body stands over.

New Year 1970

All the busted chairs out in the streets
getting iced no good for anyone anymore

all my footprints of the 60's across N.Y.C.'s sidewalks
gone, so important now I realize as if a head
was beaten in every inch of that zonked pathway

the 60's with its death of poetry
Frank O'Hara and Jack Kerouac
dead too in the pavement Olsen
dying quick moment now uptown
all last night without morphine
and why? "When it's hopeless,
give it to him, don't hesitate,"
I told Billy once, "no one works
it out on nerve when there's no nerve left."

and his is gone now, in the end

Charles Olsen

his long white hair in Gerard's photo
and my visions of Melville on looking

soon under pavement too, the rain-
soaked mattress against the stoop
shivering on 12th waiting for my man

"You better take that long pause about now . . ."

anyway everything's been driven away
and the heart has faded slightly like a tower

as you move

wasted presence
like a woods of ice
glaringly inhibited
for every new sign of the sun.

Midnight

The ambulance passes
we sit up

pinned eyes of nuns that genuflect between stars
ambassadors on marble staircases in steam tropics

and the cracked fingers of sculptured virgins
reaching out . . .

I sit cross-legged on dead trees
that float like a saint's ghost I

watch genius natives grow insane by night
juggle fire out from their veins as babies

play astral chords on water stones, breathe
lovely notes lightly, make animals dream, I fade

Prell

Day changes from cannon to morning glory
her body dances death dances in the prell light

beads strung out all through Japan's public park's, my head,
light green eyes of the birds that break branches to build homes
    there.

she tore the page, "Varieties of Emeralds"
from little sister's picture encyclopedia.

I watched this all with a spike in my vein from a top floor window
I felt the blood pass from my arm into the glass tube above it . . .

then it was rainy bonzais everywhere for me
and black masses across my brain like planets on solar maps

paper secrets I used to believe lined the open closet shelves
her body split and floated into the air forests like astral monkeys.

It's there, the air the body the soft green day:
your life cutting through the light noise of New York City's traffic
    dawn.

Back Home

Sick morning . . . school kids
playing soccer in the past
thin shaftways of graceful nostalgia
touch down my brain
sky nails falling . . .
seals silver coffin
at last and
I am happy and breathing sweat as
coils of pinkish heat make my brain sleepy I sail

over your bubble cities and watch
with secret eyes the money stomping and
great buildings rise like an empty syringe
filling with the glassy blood one thousand . . .
secretaries and vice presidents on and on
wasted energy beings with hearts
that dream of their lover's spit . . .
compressed nights in bars and toolshops
complex as a pill

as I drift
like the tongues of your patron saints
through liquid planets and ghost stars
abandoned by the children, back home . . .

who signal now to greet me
before I was born

For Sue's Birthday

There is a wind on 91st St. all night

                        (very simple wind)

it simply blows up here
to apt. 10S

          opens our windows
shakes my nose

               and says, "wake up, idiot, wake up,"

And now I've woken up.

(hello little moth,
    landing on the yellow primrose
    there on the corner table,

        stay here all winter if you like

        stay warm,

        so when summer comes
        you can get back in the open again

           fly a little above the hassles
                   so to speak,

      touch someone else now and then

                  (simple idea)

and can we join you,
           little moth,
      will you wait for us?

Down from the ceiling flies a heart
          which gracefully lands on my sleeve:

▪

and now we are young again
returning home at lunchtime
three of us
beginning everyday
to breathe the mystery
which has somehow lead us "here"

how did we get "here"?
                    what happened?

we're in a giant meadow now
our legs crossed on a sofa
we shiver from the week-old snow
which leans against our thighs
as a flower would rest beside a watermill

        which is overflowing with some incredible joy
                            onto our eyes.

Sue, I think I'll just stare at it awhile
        because out there the reservoir is so filled
        and morning touches over it like a dancer:
                            yellow and naked and wet.

        and Sue
                I think you should know
                that two people who love you so very much
                are caring for you an awful lot lately

        especially on the day that you were born:

                            which is simply today.

which is why I'm writing this poem,
                —especially for you.

Song

In minute gestures
        that jet wetly slight
   right above your eyes
            each morning
I watch the sun cross over the reservoir
     all day sometimes
        a few hours soaked into air cotton
like cloud syringes drawing up blue
          like darkness when it's through

Poem

This country invades me

and you can join me

             if you know . . .

I feel   an uneasy warmth
blue mist of grass fingers   gliding thru my pulse
that clear abandoned infants
from the day's movements
                their strange eyes

rushes of pure summer
that later form energy tulips

they polish eyes
in light ballets
           that hum

I begin
      to sing
          to its sway

the warmth   shoots
                light missiles
                   of blue oxygen

thru my lungs
         you know . . .

those babies breathe
too heavy
                  strange eyes

air that shatters into sweet inspiration

Love Story

The penalty for desertion
is death by a firing squad.

I'm saving you this trouble

enclosed is a pistol.
loaded with only one bullet.
squeeze the trigger once
perhaps nothing will happen.

but squeeze a second time . . .
a third time . . .   You see

I know the games you love

In This Room Particularly

I wake to move easy

                              (a sacred heart
                              carved in wood
                              rests over my shoulder)
with a sense that

through this Japanese garden
                              (my head)
laced with plums falling
noiseless and unbruised
                                    in my head

you see
                    you're the one . . .

will be stuck
among those branches

                    I created
                                    up there

too strong

for a long time to pass

thru the river in your view in my head

The Tenth Try

I owe a lot to someone
I've watched her tear
fall like an icarus
it was like a star
which is the sun
who is me.

it won't be long
that I will look up
and feel the sounds again
that I pretend sometimes
that they are gone forever.

the steps are simple
to walk in this universe
you must feel each one distinct
as if someone had died
their faces designating each constellation.

you realize
what connects that time you spent
lying on the lawn you remember
is not so long before
and, say, the beauty of the statue
you saw last monday an angel there
her lips hung over the garden, the stone garden.

that connection
is not so easy finding it
in one's mind
and yet the solution
is but a clue . . . the garden, the stone garden . . .
to all you have meant to me
and why this is so.

Love Poem
for Cassy

I see myself, sad now, as in a mirror
appearing before us sad now as in a movie that lies.

I am sick of N.Y.C. but I hate
adobe huts and sad communes
with naked girls carrying hunting knives
nailed to their sides 10,000 ft. above Manhattan.

so I walk
down gloomy Park Ave South early morning
in my head one more time
with its dawn churches
with their stained glass dripping
like your eyes I see
before me in a mirror
waking slowly in daylight.

For Your Birthday
for D.C.

It is right
to be exactly the way it is
where even the sun won't begin
runs fast away
birds gather specks of white petals
and leave them in circles for the nuns to watch
when they pass the window to greet / the paths
this morning

                                and that happens every day this time

let me tell you
that I have survived all
I have seen through windows . . .
I formed no ideas except that one . . .
that one like the story of the man and hunter
that night shaking hands in the wintry inn
was he leaving or had he just arrived?

                        night surrounded by star streams like gauze.

and I've avoided
the image that my heart
might some other time recall
although at times the wind advances into the nest
which hides the metals and cakes they have all presented me

what I wanted
was a narrow room
filled with simple love and exact emotions
no symbols and no dreams
one notion two might survive forever
though we will not always believe it, after all,

the rain gathers the stones always

and in winter
the stones are eyes

their dim freeze holding

Poem

Yesterday you past
into your lips . . . your hips
and your breasts
a poor unconsummated memory

we spent sick days
was tragic sometimes
sometimes was silly

but sometimes it was on a sweet log
on a long walk after dinner
in your windy warm energy jeans

fingers touching.

On the Rush

I stuck out my palm . . .
the snow the pine needles
hit lightly

I thought it was rain for a minute
I thought the game had been called

Words from Babylon

Africa is bleeding
from the rape of her light

all black men are thus
those who are ambivalent toward her

here in Babylon
our hands revolutionize
and make green
love

and then?

and then?

Torn Canvas

A man passes through a gate
as wide as his eyes

his wife stands before it thirteen hours
she waits

she cries

The Birth and Death of the Sun

Now the trees tempt
the young girl below them

each moves off the other's wind
endlessly, as stars from the earth,

stars from the stars.

It Doesn't Matter

Though the phonograph got melted and the radio
is angry sounds, yawning mammal stampedes at dawn

sounds . . . you know? because I'm far down in the insect
sweat where underfed honey cherubs clog my ears . . .

whisper over our fates . . . theirs: leukemia . . . mine: poetry
its possibilities . . . like the young girl signaling

at the water's edge, gate to music cool as green insect
wings rise up from down's sweaty pools; my eyes

jackhammer through the fog up to clear space, walk out
to the watery gate, music fixed up in surf, ends the poem . . .

seals my fate.

Chelsea May

A pair of frozen dice come
tumble through picture windows
the sun slips out and
she is standing at the gate
with all her possibilities

I conceal so much
moving in and out poetry
I could have simply left a note
tell you how I hate
getting up each morning and
drink coffee, feel unslightly sick and . . .

What Coleridge couldn't admit, well,
DeQuincey, he cashed in on it.

do you see,
                    Chelsea May?

it's just a feeling I have at times
I want to live until I want to die
and I don't want their cures
no matter what I say
my mind is shot into storms
and she's leaning on the gate etc. . . .

Savage Bubbles

for Carol Kane

You shift
into lonely music
trail fading emeralds and cocaine leopards

■ ■ ■

I snag you raw
at snake games in white rooms
smashed windows
like babies afraid of colors

■ ■ ■

These leopards are animal proud
sexy quick   astral masters
of jungle nights, frozen
dramas in the camera's eye,
blink . . . ocean rush . . . dawn rests on us
the pads of your eyes

■ ■ ■

Sleep
to sleep
to sleep inside insect ballets
to sleep in landscapes
on painted doors, icy windows

■ ■ ■

Great morning of Plan Zoo
we gather to break bars
crush cages, dawn streaked
like the mandrill's stare, we free
eaters of meat to the city plazas

■ ■ ■

I fade
into your vibes
we skate Fifth Ave.
on its frozen fear

(You can make suns rise
　　Incredible brain surf!

　　It happens!
　　　　　　　　Savage bubbles)

　　　　　■ ■ ■

Breathe still
huddled dreams for softness
kitten bellies flow
ear to ear
where long hair lay

　　　　　■ ■ ■

That's another
city dream on waking with
your gypsy eyes
uncombed with
your ankles raised
like flags

Paregoric Babies

Clocks blue seconds fold over me
slow as swamp dreams I feel
heavy like metal shade pre-dawn thickness

                                                 I sit

in my chair of nods shivering
from a sickness I took years to perfect

dark paddling in the wave membrane
the monkey woman's dream streams
are places of shy creatures, head infants
I had born on a whim and abandoned . . . my eye

drips the strain in the sweet March air, frozen
pure as my blood refuses to flow . . .
stilled, sweat that shines the breath of my poem

An Apple at Dawn

The orange in side walk

                                is shivering
is morning   light
        near the park   a tree
opening up   sparkling breakfasts

        a couple of million

moving people   moving along
into the grace of victories

                                        in the air
                                        a finger

in the water   a face
        your own
and others   a french schoolgirl
        for one   humming on a bus

                a breeze assembled

in your fist   a voice rehearsing
in your lap   because lately "you get"

                (the wing lift mildly:
                        they're COLD AND ENDURING
your body is pumping:
                        it is filled with blood.

you don't really feel totally useless,

                        do you?

                and you're occasionally aware.

.

. . . these stringy clouds   look out Manhattan

       your prince's sorrow

   might be back   again   tomorrow.

The Book of Nods

To Rosemary & Ted

Trained Monkey

I'm a trained monkey. You don't see many of us anymore,
though the streets of the larger cities were once filled with us.
Who is to say why we have nearly passed, like several of my
cousin species of the jungle and rain forest, into extinction?
Some say we were no more than a fad and like all fads were
bound to pass, that it is no longer charming to see us dance as
our masters grind out music from an old and far-off country.
But I am a living, breathing thing, and find it abusive to be so
labeled.

I would have you know that I am part of a prestigious line
of trained monkeys. My grandpapa worked in the movies from
the time he was taken from his own mother's breast. He was
the one who swirled at his master's feet, as he played a
mournful dirge in an exquisite dance of foreboding, as Law-
rence Tierny (playing the gangster John Dillinger) walked to
that final movie with the traitorous woman in red. My own
mother appeared often on the stage in what has come to be
called the Golden Age of Television, before she was sold by
her trainer, a scoundrel and drunkard, to a life in the streets,
dancing, as I still dance, for the coins of children and the
good working people returning from their lunch breaks. We
worked together through my early years . . . oh, truly it was
the most wonderful time of my life.

I recall with the greatest detail the way she would lovingly
swat me across the head as I scuffled across her path on the
pavement, the way she would teach me, with such patience,
the secrets of certain acrobatic stunts which some experts
would have you believe are inherent characteristics to our spe-
cies. (Believe me, they are not inherent, but very much ac-
quired skills . . . for example, have you ever seen a relative of
mine, among the trees and trellises of his natural jungle envi-
ronment, do somersaults on the seat of a bicycle as his mama
pedals from the chrome guard above the back wheel?) More
than any of this, I remember the touch of her small, pink fin-
gers as she groomed me at night, tugging my ear with her
tight lips, and, once again, the loving swat, signaling she was
finished, that I should sleep.

With van Gogh

I am sitting on a park bench in the neighborhood where I was
raised as a boy. Van Gogh approaches me in the dark, a wide
blue gash laid down his luminous cheeks. There are some
thin papers folded beneath his arms, secured by a ribbon. He
is wearing a cheap iridescent suit, beneath it a yellow polo
shirt with the image of two small green alligators copulating
sewn on above the pocket. Over his spiked red hair is a felt
hat, its wide brim covered with twelve thick candles. They are
burning rapidly in the wind and give off the scent of a cathe-
dral. There is no reason I should know who he is, but I do.
He tells me he is going down beyond the running track to
paint the Harlem River. I ask him to sit awhile and talk with
me, and in a crippled fashion he lowers himself beside me on
the bench. I notice the famous missing ear and he sees this
and anticipates a question—"It was an experience, right?"—
and he laughs. We are both laughing. We cannot stop laugh-
ing . . . we are bent over with our fists pounding our guts and
howling into the wind as it grows. Just then a woman in a
dark dress approaches us in tears. Van Gogh looks up to her,
as if to ask, "Why are you doing this?" The woman explains
that she has come tonight to realize so many contradictions in
her life, that her entire life seems a contradiction and that she
is unable to bear such a notion and so has been weeping all
through the evening and, now, into the night. Van Gogh and
I look to each other and slowly build into even greater fits of
laughter. He is pointing up at the woman and clutching my
knee and his shoulders are bouncing up and down in hyster-
ics. The woman cries harder, as if for her tears to outdo our
laughter. Seeing this, van Gogh rises. Standing before her, he
mutters slowly the phrase, "My many contradictions . . . my
many contradictions . . ." over and over; then he closes his
fist and smashes the woman across the face with incredible
force. As the woman, who I see now is quite beautiful, goes
down to the pavement, van Gogh falls back beside me on the
bench and looks at me, laughing. Then he looks down at the
woman and speaks, "There, now you really have something
to cry about!" He looks back over to me, after a moment of

silence, and we begin laughing again. I throw my arms around him and lay my head to his shoulders, continuing to laugh until my tears begin to fall down the lapel of his suit, which is glowing from the fluorescent light in the lamppost above us.

A Poet Dies

I.

Those who die in my dreams have taught me well of the
modern world; I have taken from them an everlasting nobility.
And they die always in the past, where the wooden frames of
windows are too thick for my hands to grip. I hold on above
the streets and watch them, unseen from within. A young
poet has died overnight in his chained bed. His face is shaded
blue with sweet asphixiation; his eyes have left their sockets
and roll back and forth across the shivering floorboards, as if
gravity were upset for the absurdity of his death. His lips are
black and thick like a painted whore. The lymph stones are
sinking beneath his throat. It is all too much for the bearded
doctor, who wipes the condensation from his eyeglasses and
draws a stunning white hood from his bag to cover the poet's
head. He hands the certificate of death to the hotel owner and
the chamber girl to sign. I hear the young girl, who alone is
saddened by the beautiful dead man beside her, tell the doc-
tor that she is able to write, but has no name. He takes the
certificate from her trembling hand with impatience and marks
it with an X beneath the hotel owner's signature. A sheet is
raised over the hooded body and the three withdraw from the
room. I can hear the doctor's laughter trailing down the hall-
way. I look down once more to the floor, where the poet's
eyes have come to rest along a thin dull carpet. They are
fixed on me, blue and clean.

II.

Only for those who die am I naked in my dreams, and be-
cause he has died so young, my body outside his window is
flawless and thin. Some men in finely cut suits in the streets
below are upset by this. They scream up to me in German;
they think it is important I know that they are lawyers. And
they send some young boys at play, who thought me an
angel, around the square to bring them the magistrate. I have
no time for them, my eyes are riveted still to the floor. The

dead poet's eyes are signaling me to a table directly beneath the window. I smash the glass with my jade rings and gather up his notebooks lying there. I place them secure on the sill beside me and look back. But the eyes have dissolved, there is nothing left but some shadows of heat rising from the carpet. Somehow the whole room has changed, and the knotted blood throbbing beneath the hood and sheet is stilled. But the lawyers beneath me are screaming louder, now they are flinging small stones and bits of jagged glass. I see blood across my bare ankles, but it does not sing. I'm driven beneath compassion for those of the past; these vile little fiends, with their stiff, perfect hair and their tattooed pricks, have let their poets die unknown in chained beds. Gravity knows the justice of my revenge, and comes to my aid. I dance on the ledge, with the notebooks of a dead poet between my legs. I wrap my naked body in some blinding foil, and the sun scatters off me in thin lines like wires whose heat slits the lawyers' eyes. Some grey fluid runs from the holes. They cup their ring-laden fingers to their faces and moan and stumble to the gutter to turn on their elbows in the scum pools. I balance like a dancer on the edge and piss on each of them eternal syphilis through the slits, before the cure has been given. I tighten the notebooks beneath my arms for my return, and look down. I will have no more from them . . . I am of the future, and my power is great.

Homage to Gerard Manley Hopkins

Passing through customs was a fast and pleasant experience, not at all what I had anticipated. This was, after all, the capital of a land still reverberating from the shockwave of revolution, and my country, though maintaining relations in a formal sense, was spoken of only in the most hostile terms. Its citizens no longer clung blindly to the rail of oblivion without resistance, led by that banished dictator who deposited so many, by his own hand or through those of his agents, into the abyss. Their eyes seemed wide open now; they embraced the revolutionary council as true brothers of their salvation. The exceptions were few, and holed up in the hills near the border. Their only source of weapons and, indeed, of clothing and food came from the covert aid of my own country. So visitors such as myself are viewed at best as intruders and, more likely, as outright enemies. I wondered, then, why I was passed through the customs line with no search of my baggage and a few perfunctory questions. I'd had much more difficulty crossing the border into Canada last winter, when I was made to remove the spare tire from the trunk of my car so that the inspectors might search among the oily rags and check the insulating lining of an ice chest.

It was true I was here as a guest of a government office, at the invitation of the committee for cultural events. I am a writer and translator; I hold an esteemed post in the comparative literature department of a most prestigious university. Still, I was taken back by the remarkable efficiency of the finely dressed men (three, no less) who greeted me immediately upon retrieving my baggage. They guided me quickly to a car whose engine was already open. No sooner had I touched my body to the spacious back seat than we were weaving throughout the crosshatched traffic, whose cars always seem smaller and unfamiliar in foreign places. Looking closer through the open window, however, I realized these were, after all, quite different from any autos I had seen at home or in my many years of travel. Picking up on my curiosity, one of the agents, who was facing me from a jumpseat, explained how all imports had been banned within the last three months, as far as the automobile industry was concerned. "But, of course, you would know all about such affairs," he whispered enigmatically, his face contorted without any apparent effort into what was, literally, a half smile and half sneer, each side opposing the other like a composite photograph. I replied, puzzled and somewhat anxious, that I had no idea what he meant, then hastened to loosen up the atmosphere of these close quarters . . . which seemed to be growing closer still . . . by commenting how amazing the cars looked and what a genuine feat it must have been to produce them. I fell short of expressing my considered opinion of just how terribly ugly these cars were. There were, from what I'd seen, two uniform models, which did, in their defense, offer exactly twice the variety of Hitler's vision for a vehicle to transport citizens of the fatherland. Both models were hideous. One looked like a shoe. The other was larger, shaped in almost the exact proportions of a coffin. Each had wheels smaller in circumference and width than that of a standard motorcycle, which seemed, right there, to be a failing proposition to even a layman's eyes. From the sounds which enclosed us on either side, it was obvious nobody around the drawing board had considered including mufflers in the design. The sound was deafening; the highway more like a lake during a race for those cigar-shaped, monstrous powerboats. Our own vehicle, I suddenly realized, was more like a sailboat, icily quiet, a leftover import from the old days of the new regime, or, more likely, the early days of the old regime. It was, in fact, an old British Daimler, very much in mint operating condition. Why did I rate an anomaly? The cultural people seemed to put a higher estimate on my work than I myself did, even in my wildest frenzy of ego beneath the halfway point of a fifth of Scotch. I looked closer at my companions; it was a questioning stare that went unanswered. None of them looked at all Latino in feature; they all looked quite the same. The car, I noticed, was getting cold. Not cool, but cold. My companions' breathing grew visible. I was breathing too thinly to give off a sign.

Things began to happen quickly then. Both back windows came up at once, powered by a remote up front. It must have been installed specially; this car predated such devices. The windows were darkly tinted. I could see nothing from them but the reflections of the others and myself, so the space grew even smaller. That's when the fellow opposite me, with the same clashing expression, began to speak. The others moved in tighter and leaned forward; the three tracks of icy breath met and mingled between them in a single small cloud which rose to the ceiling and dissolved. "Sir," he asked in the same whispering tone, "are you familiar with the works of a poet of your own language, a poet by the name of Gerard Manley Hopkins?"

"Yes, of course," I answered, amazed at the question. "A fine poet, and a favorite of mine in my undergraduate days. He was a priest, you know."

"Oh, but indeed I do know," the man, his menace growing, replied, "and I am grateful for your candor in this matter."

I had no idea what he was getting at. My candor about what?

Something else . . . his accent was shifting. He had spoken so little, I hadn't noticed at first the false note in his Latino phrasings of English. Now he seemed to have lapsed into a more East European tone: that methodical, Slavic slurring of words punctuated with short, clipped declaratives.

Outside the car the unmuffled engines had ceased, and I could feel that the texture of the road beneath us had changed from asphalt to dirt. We were obviously outside the city, heading deeper into the countryside. Suddenly there was a thudlike sound, and the driver slammed on his brakes. One man got out while the other two seemed to slide into what they considered to be strategic positions. They moved as casually and calmly as two who had drilled such moves many times. No more than half a minute passed before the third man had returned. He explained that we had hit an animal, and we began to move on. He did not elaborate. He did not say what kind of animal. Neither did he mention if it was killed or still alive.

"Did Hopkins write poems about animals?" I was asked by the same man as before.

"I'm afraid I don't know . . ." I hesitated.

"I don't believe he did," he went on. "And I would know. In the last two months I have read all of his works. I have read them in three languages. I have also read all available biographical material. He was not born Catholic, but converted and, ten years later, was ordained. I think he preferred trees to animals, as far as subjects for his poems . . . trees and his God."

"He had a wonderful way of blending the formal with the colloquial," I blurted back, hardly believing I had said it. I was shaking visibly now, not only from the increasing cold within the car, but from a deep anxiety with the realization that these men were neither from the ministry for culture nor, for that matter, from the country we were in.

"You seem to be shaking, sir," he cooed, draping a blanket, which was thin enough to be totally without use, around me. "And may I say that was an astute comment."

"What?"

"What you said about Hopkins . . . the formal language blended with—"

"It was hardly astute," I interrupted, "and may I ask you what the hell is going . . ."

" 'Ah, as the heart grows older,' " he recited, " 'It will come to such sights colder / By and by, nor spare a sigh / And yet you will weep and will know why . . .' "

I stared at him directly. His composure was becoming comical. I was still afraid, yet found myself angry enough to say what I was thinking. "Your game is becoming ludicrous. I refuse to be a part of it. You are obviously some sort of agents from another government. I have no idea what you want from me, but—"

"My recitation, sir." He cut me off once more. "Have you no comment to make? Please indulge me, for it seems it is more likely you who is playing the game."

"I truly don't know what you mean. As for the poem, you added an extra word in the last line. There is only one, 'will' . . . The second one was your own contribution. Also, you left out an entire line: the one next to the last. It goes, 'Though worlds of wanwood leafmeal lie . . .' Are you satisfied? Is your idiot inquiry finished? Will I be handed a grade?"

He said nothing, but knocked on the glass partition twice. The driver deftly spun the car about, and we were again heading back toward the city. "I'm sorry for the inconvenience, sir," he finally spoke, this time in another accent, decidedly British, "but, you know, we had to be certain. I'm sure you understand, though you played the role with amazing conviction . . . certainly much better than our rather melodramatic East Bloc routine. Now, here is the envelope containing the documents. Your plane tickets are included as well. We'll be returning you to the hotel at the airport now. You'll need sleep; your flight leaves early."

The contorted face had relaxed into something else. He was still quite an unattractive man, and I was glad to be rid of him and his companions when they dropped me at the hotel. I burned the envelope without opening it, flushing the ashes down the toilet. Then I slept.

I never contacted anyone from the ministry of culture, and flew out the next morning, glad to miss the conference. One would think such a strange experience would deeply affect my life. It has not. I've forgotten it . . . in any real sense, that is. I will offer one piece of advice, however: Never learn too well the works of a poet, for, somehow, the works of the masters have infiltrated the systems of those who are dangerous and covert. They have turned lines of beauty and love into codes of identification. Security is maintained in the detection of a flawed meter, and messages of coercion and betrayal are delivered in iambics.

Watching the Schoolyard

It is a decade now past my decadence. My beast wears rings and he hides under the shadows of my silent hesitations. Each image is so clear, yet I have no hands to adore the precision. The finest gestures of the air are traced on my eyelids. I see them and they see me, but there is never a reply. No hollow flash when the light withdraws, leaving with it a crevice where the angel signals, only to begin again.

Still, I think I have moved closer to my heart. Sometimes I sit near a window and watch kids at recess in the schoolyard. They are passing around some thin girl's false eye. They inspect it with a magnifying glass which, I assume, one of them has stolen from his father's desk. When I see them finally give it back and run to the fountain to carefully wash their hands and dry them on their starched shirtsleeves, I realize the eye is quite real. As real as each one's nonchalance, walking back to their games. It could have been a jewel.

They gather in a circle and a leather ball is flung toward the sky. Their thin hands hold back the sun from their sight. But for them, in that shadow, something else moves. And suddenly each one is gone. The ball remains, as if poised on a stream of air. Things are beginning to seem like symbols for my losing control. My cat pumps its hind legs twice, and leaps into the mirror. I need someplace to hide. I undo my belt buckle and tie it tight. I hear a train passing over dried-up waters. I watch stunned heat snap the cold wings of birds.

When I withdraw the point and untie my belt, the thin young girl returns. She comes to my open window with her eye in her palm, extending it to me. It could have been a jewel. It's so real. It makes me feel so human. There are tired lines at the edges, thin and magenta like an insect's veins. But I don't want to look at it; I want to hear it. I hold it to my ear. I hear the calm voice of a woman, whispering some words of love and caution. It must be the girl's mother. It is lovely; I look down to her. Morning has never meant so much as her Christian smile, the perfect weight of her small, wet fingers, as light like crushed glass strains through their crevices.

Guitar Voodoo

I awakened in a pool of mild chemical reaction. I stood up
then in the darkness and felt what it was drain slowly from
my ankles and fingertips. It felt like thousands of lesser hands
weaving small flags beneath my skin. The darkness of that
room hummed like a small machine; there was a thin red glow
shining from the walls. Turned and noticed some strips of
fluorescent light outline a doorway. Felt along there for a
switch . . . there was a button, instead, shaped like a V. I
saw I was in a photographer's darkroom. The liquid I had
woken in, now almost totally dissolved across my skin, must
have been some agent used in the developing process. I
searched over myself to check for damaging effects. There
were no burns, apparently, though my veins glowed a
metallic silver. I ran my forearms under some warm water,
but it only seemed to sharpen the effect. I figured I'd come
back to it later. I began to take a look around. I found a
drawer in a metal cabinet with my lover's name on it. I
forced the lock and withdrew the contents, a box of color
slides she had once taken of her ex-husband. There were a
dozen of them, each with the same pose of him leaning naked
against the trunk of a lavender Bentley. They obsessed me
immediately. I emptied them into my jacket pocket and
returned the box to the drawer, leaving it open. Pushed
another V-shaped button and took an eight-seat jet back to
the city.

I never liked this man. I once read in my lover's diary the
methods he used in bed to please her. What I read haunted
me many months; it reached such clarity beneath my eyes
when I lay beside her in the darkness that for sixteen weeks I
could not bring myself to know her skin. It forced her to re-
turn to him each Sunday morning, and when I discovered
this, I led her out one evening to the beryllium flats and with
a shovel dug a place for her to rest. When the time came that
I wanted her back, I realized she had many months before
forgotten how to breathe.

I know guitar voodoo. I learned it from a woman with white hair in the hills above Kingston, who all day slit open the crowns of oranges and raised them above her head for the sun to drink. At night, one day each month, she gathered the dry, pale skins in mounds and left them for the full moon to push back beneath the earth. The cycle gave her great powers, and because I one day taught her the proper way to sharpen the blade on her knife, she gave some power to me.

She opened the case of my guitar and placed six fingertips to the pickups beneath the strings. She made a tea from the dried orange skins on her fire, and taught me the way of guitar voodoo. When I got to my apartment with the photographs, I placed them in a plain glass bowl. I lifted from my dresser the porcelain sphere the white-haired mistress had given me one year past. The scent from the thick golden substance inside was sweet and true like a child breathing . . . this was a by-product of what the sun itself had one day left behind for me. With my adrenaline rising, a slow heat turned like a fist beneath my heart. My hands tightened for the power. I poured the substance into the bowl, over the squares of processed celluloid containing his image. When the last drop rolled out, I put down the sphere and, though it served no purpose for the ceremony, I danced one hour before I slept.

By the time I woke next morning the magic was already complete. I shaved to make myself pretty. I went to the living room sofa; I took the slides from the bowl and laid them in two rows of six across the glass tabletop. I raised the bowl to my lips and drank what was left over. Opened the closet door and removed my guitar from its case. Turned the power on with the switch on the amp and hooked the jacks. I shut my eyes as the potion took me over. There were small globes the color of burst capillaries, framed by an uncertain gravity before a white expanse . . . then an image began to focus. I could see, clearly as the sun, the man who was my lover's husband, lying in bed in his home in northern California. He was just waking. Some shadows of morning light hung from the brass bedposts. He was sitting up now beneath a fancy quilt with his eyes fully opened. I took one of the voodoo slides, turned rigid by the potion overnight, and, fingering on the neck of the guitar an "A" chord, ran his naked image across the strings.

I saw the reaction as if standing behind a mirror on his bedroom wall. His body shuddered violently on the bed. He seemed to be pulled a few inches off the mattress until the sound finally quit reverberating inside the amp. The room was left with a hollow ringing within silence, like air inside a nitrous oxide dream. He gripped his convulsing and stopped it. His eyes searched the room for answers. He checked some objects on top of the bookshelves, praying with moving lips they had been knocked over to sustain his hope that there was an earthquake taking place. But nothing was moved. I was delirious with pleasure. I upped the volume of the amp to "8" and ran the voodooed image across the strings windmill style, like Pete Townsend. He was thrown back down across the floorboards, as if by the force of a giant reptile's tail across his neck. I couldn't figure out if the voodoo force worked from outside his body or within . . . more likely both, I imagined. He quivered on his back and implored the ceiling. On his bare chest six lines of blood, thin as guitar strings, opened and pulsed. I looked down and noticed the red draining down my fingers' crevices . . . the magic was transporting his blood to me. I thought a moment to stop it, but it was out of my control. I slammed into another "G" chord. I saw a woman run into his room and gape in astonishment. When I saw her hands clapped tight across her ears, I realized he was *screaming out* guitar chords from deep inside his lungs, with the same volume produced by my guitar and amp. His larynx about to shatter like a crystal goblet.

More chords . . . he slammed against four walls. He was weakening; my power was growing stronger. His fingers clutched his throat for the pain each uncontrolled shriek was causing. The veins along his forearms were throbbing and choking each other like killer vines. The woman bolted from the room, signing herself with the cross. I realized it was beginning to do him in . . . the building tension of the strings in "E" forced the lines of blood across his chest to spurt like steam from split valves. And it was bringing sounds from within him which human tissue was incapable of bearing. I slapped my hand across the pickups to snuff the sound. I wiped the sweat and blood from the glass tabletop and leaned over to switch off the power in the amp. There was a last image of his body dropping limp and unconscious to the stunned floorboards of his room. I opened my eyes. I undid my belt buckle. And slept.

My Father's Vacation

I have distilled the natural world into a clear clean liquid, so I no longer need to think about it. When I'm there I am contained on all sides by water, what I move through cannot touch me. And the air I breathe is within my veins, as the fire there creates its own wind, on the rush. I don't run, I barely walk before I reach my destination. It's all just so much insulation . . . when the first bombs are whistling overhead, men will be frantic searching for a means to keep out death from their walls. They'll have to rediscover dirt. Junkies have it now, this inscrutable facade. Nothing and no one unasked for gets through the door.

The fact that it's all dropping down the big tube is so much melodrama to me. The reports nightly on the evening news, with their eager visuals of the planet unraveling, might as well be reruns of *Green Acres* to me. I no longer concern myself with cancer. I watch reactors erected through a glass screen in living color. How could it be possible they are just up the Hudson River, no more than an hour's drive away? When my father's vacation came around each summer, when I was a kid, we'd drive an hour in that very direction to swim in a pool with fourteen diving boards. And what if it is there? What if it's somewhere else, on all sides, as they say "Going up?" in the trade? I watch it in color . . . to be honest, I can't even say I'm oblivious to the real *beauty* of processed uranium, to the light blue glow of fissionable rods under water. I imagine it emits a pretty hum, like the reverberation deaf children hear when a tuning fork is placed against their earbones. Besides, I haven't left my room since I fell in love with guns. How can one who hasn't opened his door in three weeks fear anything?

Quality

The man that came by yesterday said our bees were the biggest he had ever seen in this county. "And the result is better quality," I added proudly, pouring the sweet honey into his tea for him to taste. My wife hands me our daughter and I place her across my knee. She does her little trick of turning her head 360 degrees on her shoulders, then giggles with restraint. She, too, is proud. This has all happened in less than two years, in fact, and before that I knew nothing about the small creatures and the manner in which they created the thick, pleasing liquid. The first time I was stung put an end to my last anxiety, and now I accept an occasional sting with a patient, knowledgeable tolerance. They are for the most part so unexpectably well behaved, and it is only the passing of the jeeps and tanks through the mountain road leading to Camp Davidson that at times upsets them, irritates and leaves them the worse for a short while in the way of production. We couldn't have chosen a more exciting crop and, judging from the miracles it works on our breakfast toast, a more rewarding one either.

Post Office

I.

I have to go out looking for the dog. I hear his curved whine coming from the wooded area down near the pumping station. I knew before I had arrived that the children of the farm workers had once more hung him from the wire drawn between the trees. I cut him loose with some flat broken glass. He is unharmed but shaking . . . he has been dreaming again of rising from the waters. His dreams keep him safe. He has taught me much about it.

I let him follow without the leash. I must make it to the post office before the siren signals noon. I run beside the highway but there is no room to get to the other side, so I hold my rings up to the sun to blind the drivers' eyes. When the traffic is still, I lower my hands and pass through. I arrive before the siren through the post office doors . . . yet the siren has been broken, some jealous women explain, and I am far too late.

II.

Today I leave the dog on the wire. His dreams will keep him safe. He dreams of the ocean; he wants to move forever without sleep, like the shark. So I reach the post office on time. I pass through the corridor and come to the box they have given me. Beside it, a beautiful doll is sleeping without air. In a corner further down, an old man in a coat which touches the floor has his eye on me. He knows I am a thief, and makes sure I take nothing that is not my own. But my patience is flawless, and I know someday he will be reassigned. Then I will steal this woman, and hang her, with the dog, from the wire. Exposed to the silver air, she will glitter. I have been in love with her since I came to this town. I turn the combination to my box, but there is nothing inside.

III.

I have been here too long. The doll is gone. The man in the
long coat has taken her place. The dog is dead. He stopped
dreaming and drowned on the wire. I had a card in the mail
this morning, the same as each day this week. It is a faded
blue and white, like Giotto's sky, emblazoned with pure gold
leaf. It reads, "Our Lady of the Immaculate Conception
would like to invite you to a meeting with your assassin." I
laughed until the man behind the glass began to awaken.
Without the dog, I can take or leave it.

The Ice Capades

It is deep winter, I am sitting on a dead tree with my guardian, staring down across the pearly blue ice on the pond. Some guitar chords, like claws from a distant balcony, have scratched in the ice the figures of popes, centuries old. They are dressed so neatly, in gold iridescent suits. The crowns they wear are not the crowns of Peter, but of a leader of some bellicose Moorish tribe. I write some words on flat white hair and glide it across the frozen surface like crushed lilies. Darkness curves over the project roofs and draws lines across the thousand pious faces. The ashes from burnt incense have dulled the reflections along the edges of the pond. Some young boys in liturgical gowns are lighting huge candles set in mounts of gold and lapis. Neither my guardian or I are in any way awed by what is taking place. I once fell through this ice. I know what it can do.

My guardian's dog comes to my hand to feed. Then he takes up the razor between his teeth and glides across the skull of our holy fathers to free the stranded insects. One named Leo climbs the steps of a makeshift pulpit. As he begins to speak, a bright orange scum flows down from the drains above his frozen teeth. It flows down the pulpit steps like gasoline, until a candle slips from the hands of an altar boy as he signs himself with the cross. And flames rise to chase the screams across frozen water.

"The Academy of the Future Is Opening Its Doors . . ."

—John Ashbery

On the nod it was five-thirty and the minutes rushed beyond their standard progression, so that each doubled . . . and what was left doubled again. Anyone knows that if you take a penny and double it daily, one to two to four to eight to sixteen, etc. . . . within a month that man would be a millionaire. When time begins to work this way, as it seems to more and more with each nod these days, the results are devastating.

So it was horrible. The Academy was offering a pot-luck dinner in my honor, and my date and I were already terribly late. To make matters worse, I brought the salad but realized on exiting the cab, under the Plaza's heated veranda, I had forgotten our special dressing . . . (paregoric, sesame oil, and crushed lentils). My date gets upset when I talk about it.

You would think that was enough blundering for one day, no matter how time was moving. But I couldn't resist the sky, and my head began to rise. Then, with a slow rush, my lips began to bleed. All over the salad it flowed, and an equal amount on my formal wear.

Now the Academy chairman has appeared through revolving doors. He walked down lucite steps to take my hand. It was the only time I could recall both his hands being empty. He took me aside and whispered into my mouth, his tongue pressed to mine, "You had better go back, we can always do this again some other time."

I thanked him for his consideration and slid back into the cab, exposing thigh-high boots beneath my robe. The chairman deftly ascended the stairs, two by two. He handed the teakwood bowl to the startled doorman, who licked traces of blood from the salad.

Parting the Reeds

I.

I lie drugged along the banks of the Nile. The tall reeds are like fingers, signaling me to the pleasures of death by water. I pass into the tide. I straddle an ancient crocodile and, with the spikes upon my tongue, lick the soft green algae of one hundred years from its neck. He takes me under, the light there is blue as the ceiling of a Cuban church.

II.

My chest has been slashed in lines thin as razors, by wires of light from the summit of a pyramid. I lie twisting on a slab of stone darkened by moss and the shadows of evening. A young boy in pillbox hat comes and pads my wounds with mud from the Nile. He wears no shirt, the flesh across his belly is scarred and stretched. He tells me of the time he climbed to the eye of Cheops and was drenched by tears of acid and scented oil. I notice an old man to his right, drinking from the shoreline through a hollow reed. His eyes are red and white, and twice the size of the boy's or mine. As he moves toward us, I see he is blind. The boy leans to me and whispers of a time the old man was led away by a ruler for words he had written in his youth. They removed his eyes with prongs in the desert and fed them to some pitted snakes. Then he was led to the river, to the place we now stand over, and he was given the eyes of a crocodile. From that day, he turns to this very place each evening and plays music through an instrument whose voice resembled the sound of an ocarina.

The Lakes of Sligo

She was speaking into the telephone in the cracked glass
booth across the street from The Lakes of Sligo saloon, down
the block from Needle Park. She fingered more and more
dimes through the tubes and they slid until my bell began to
ring. I was lying in bed with a burnt spoon messing the
sheets. And there was water spilling. The idea of heaven
seemed a bit too simple . . . then again, there was no reason
it shouldn't be just that. If the stars are milked. If the angels'
bones are hard and sharp like badly split diamonds. She is
speaking now on the telephone, asking for more time. I don't
have a phone. I hear her speaking nonetheless. And I see
each word as if they were colors from the phantom's lips. Out
the window I watch a taxi passing by a woman with a shiny
cane on Broadway. Six Temple elders feed the single pigeon
the dried wafer in islands between the traffic. Another try
with the needle through the fungus like a nightshade mush-
room on my thigh. There is some mean gravity waiting be-
neath that flesh. Nothing is happening. At all.

So I cannot answer it . . . you see, I have no phone. I've
tried to convince you. I want you to know I can feel it, cruis-
ing down my spine. Like the sharp blue light of wheels be-
neath the earth. Cannot answer. Cannot win. Always and only
just sit and watch.

She knows this. She expects no reply. She says she wants
to take the ride, but she needs to find herself. She knows I
watch out for her. And she knows I'm watching now. She
opens the door of the booth with flair, and sinks her eyes to
each soft breast, where she unzips the shield and folds it
open. So I might see the blue crevice surrounding her nip-
ples, which rise like infant fingers out of clean ice.

Lenses

Each night she comes to me, places the glass from her eyes
into a small green box with mirrors. Music down the living
darkness begins. Some low-eyed Rastafarians, fingers sharp
and gleaming as the knives inside suns, enter the room in
lines. They lay hands like machetes across steel drums and
chant the deep orange. There is power there is sweetness
there is parallel light.

Within her heat, the glass above the bed turns to violent
water and I lift her up the moment before the drowning. I set
her loose. I pull her back again. No one knows none of them
could ever know. It is not for learning or love, these dreams
and their actions. It is our way of surviving.

When it is finished, the chanters throw their headdress into
the hollow flux. They take up flutes and strings to give music
to exhaustion. The speed of each dream can turn on me then
under these rapid lids. The symbols of elements pass by me;
it is only some clever women in disguise. Their bones are so
sharp; they can break through their own excuses. And we
sleep when the music is done, with our wrists resting in the
holes their children have dug beside us in the sand.

A Beach Landing

Pictures in a thick time-stained sky . . . a ship moving out.
All the sailors are plenty happy, wide grafted faces winking to
the little galley helper. Even on the shore, none of the wives
crying, they're all just slapping backs and swinging to and fro
tweed baskets filled with everything needed to get well quick.
There's a few Indians under shawls on the nod across a thin
patch of beach. Sailor's wife offers Indian a basket: "No
thanks, just nod good enough." Back on the ship, the crew
still smiling. A rack of pork meat out drying. It's a nice ship,
gold knobs on every door. The cargo they will carry is one of
candles and books, and the crew is enthused . . . they will
read all night. But one sailor looks horrible. "All the others
are happy," he speaks, "but I feel hideous." He goes to the
captain, sitting with his hand dangling across the chair's arm,
like Christ . . . or Sherlock Holmes. Certainly a wise pos-
ture . . . a wise man. And he *is* Christ-like. He signals the
sick sailor to the door; the sad man is lowered in a leather har-
ness into a small rowboat and taken back to shore, the second
year in a row this has happened.

Zeno's Final Paradox

I am resting on the glimmering salt flats, sewing emblems on
my endurance. There is a malignant smoke pouring from the
summits of distant mountains; shreds of warm asbestos settle
across my chest. I follow the flight of a single vulture into a
stranded cloud. My eyes are dry and cracked, like this desert
surface surrounding me on all sides with no end within my vi-
sion. An old Greek man named Zeno pulls up on a rocket
sled and lectures me on motion. The first step, he insists, can
never be taken . . . for half the distance will always remain
ahead. Neither time, speed, nor unyielding endurance can
make a difference. At each step of its ascent and fall, the
arrow in flight is dead . . . it does not move, but rests contin-
uously in progressing intervals . . . like the stars and planets
seen through some shuttering eye. "Even as it pierces the tar-
get at point center it is an illusion," he goes on, "the target
itself is a lie, and neither you nor I shall ever leave this
place."

Paraguay

It is all too white again. The sun has bars across its lids; the light reaches us in shafts. Numbers form across our breakfast. Someone speaks of a place where all the women are called "Madonna."

Keats is there at the table, drinking coffee and dark pine methadone. He won't give me a taste, it's bad because I oversleep a lot and miss the hours at the clinic. I'm in the bathroom disassembling the pipes. My wrists are strong in dreams, there is no need for tools. Keats speaks to me through the closed door, "There is no escape, you try to figure out what is inside and, with that knowledge, move around it. The birds, after all, do not touch earth until felled by disease." The last line, the one about the birds, sounded bogus to me . . . so I open the door to check. It's not Keats after all, it's my little sister and her tape recorder again. She smiles sinisterly and raises her dress to me. I return to the pipes, they are clean now and must be put back.

I fall asleep there on the blue carpet. It's Paraguay. A country where the trestles are rising and the birds pass through quickly. Along the countryside, the landscape is covered with bloodstained sombreros. The fat workers sing along with the music from speakers nailed to a white sky. They gather stones in burlap shawls and fling them like brown eyes at the dictator passing through the gates of the palace when the bridge is lowered at dawn and the sun drowns the voices of agriscientists returning to draw blood on the cattle before their children wake. But they are wakened nonetheless, with their bellies stretched like drums, sweet with poverty and infant grace. They know by the volume of the guns that I have just landed on their shores.

The Safe Corridor

I am walking along Eighth Street on my way to the East
River; there are things floating by there I want to watch. I can
hear the convicts pacing with superb dignity along the cat-
walks beneath these thin sidewalks. They work for the system
on commission, scraping jumpers from the tracks. Soon their
steel shoes will be silent with the changing of the guard.
Some take the time for prayer, using chains like rosary. Some
listen for the gathering of whores, when they masturbate their
partners to the clicking of their false eyelashes. There is a lu-
cite brick through which one can watch them; in front of the
shop selling masks from Africa. It is not advised, however; the
penalty is severe for non-officials. For their part the convicts
are never changed, they sleep leaning against the rail, like
horses. It seems cruel to some, but the facts remain . . . the
men themselves would have it no other way. The suicide ex-
change rate rises steadily, and, as was mentioned, they work
on commission.

As I reach Broadway and Eighth I realize I will get no fur-
ther on foot. When evening comes, the next block, the one
leading to Astor Place and the East Side, is impassable, rav-
aged by the gamma wind from the beryllium plants flanking
both sides. They are each forty flights, and though darkness
has not fallen, there is no light left through this narrow pas-
sage. On weekend nights, some school kids try to beat the
wind and blackness on a bet . . . none make it through with-
out two layers of skin left behind. So I enter, enter the booth
at the entrance to the safe corridor and hand the attendant my
card.

He cautions me that the corridor is sealed off from the gen-
eral public for the day because of a system inspection in prep-
aration for some dignitaries from the Middle East tomorrow. If
it's real important, he assures me, I can be issued a white suit
for passage and try to hitch a ride through on an authorized
vehicle. I decide to settle for his offer, and he runs my card
beneath a thin beam and hands it back. He unzippers the
back of a white suit, not unlike something worn at my acad-
emy while training for post-meltdown relief, and helps me

into it. When I'm completely fastened, he puts me through a detection ring and runs down the procedure for hitching passage. I wait on the southwest corner of Broadway and stick out my hand, exposing the transit badge I was issued. Before long, a flatbed truck with two fourteen-foot lead screens rising on both sides pulls up at the curb next to me. An old man is driving; he puts out his hand and I extend the badge for his edification. He sees that all is in order and gestures silently for me to board myself on the flatbed in back. As I climb on I notice an old black man already crouched in the corner, his back against the cab. I fasten myself with a strap beside him and the driver pulls out. As we move into the black wind I see the whores taunting the convicts beneath them through the lucite brick. One with huge breasts stands over it with her legs spread wide, so those under her might see.

Rimbaud Scenes

Rimbaud's Tooth Ache

Arthur had waited too long. Even the blue light of opium no
longer countered the pain. His teeth throbbed with it, like
the veins of a young soldier in the heat of a battle already
lost. He wailed alone at night in the painter's loft, until the
old man living one flight up, a pedant with dry blood between
the many crevices in his forehead, knocked on the door and
inquired what the trouble might be. Arthur, too tired to shield
himself behind his usual wit and insolence, made a gesture to-
ward the swollen jaw, and the old man insisted he accompany
the youth to a dentist he had known to be "quite reliable and
competent," and who had offices nearby. He would be by to
call on him following breakfast next morning, and, if Arthur
had no money to cover the expense, he insisted on arranging
payment himself with the dentist, who, he added, was a long-
time friend and an understanding sort.

Rimbaud could not deny the comfort he felt in the idea
that at this same time tomorrow the ache would be gone, yet
he could not help but lie back on the bed and regard the old
man as a fool. For the wailing that brought this neighbor to
his door had little to do with the pain upon his teeth. He
wailed for a young girl who sat that day by the fountain he
passed daily as he walked. Her dress was trimmed with lace,
white as the veils of children in processions back home. How
the spray from the fountain pressed the lines of sun deeper
and deeper into her hair until the light remained beyond the
cursed evening! "How will I ever dream again in daylight,"
he thought, "when I know she walks the streets of this city,
and breathes the air?" The darkness was already full as she
rose to go her way, and as she passed the bench where the
poet had set himself, he drew a ragged notebook from his vest
with great haste and pretended to read from its pages, which
were empty. And she passed right by, the last drops of light
sliding through the hair across her shoulders. At his feet. His
fingers quivered with an unbearable longing. To touch. This

was the source of the pain which the old man heard this
night, sounding through the floor beneath him.

Rimbaud Sees the Dentist

As he had promised, the old man knocked at Arthur's door
early that morning. Rimbaud was ready, and together they
passed down into the fresh blocks of sunlight on the side-
walks. Rimbaud was neatly dressed, though his frail black tie,
which was more like the lace of a boot, could not conceal the
lines of dirt along his collar.

"You should hold no fear of the pain one often takes for
granted on the way to the dentist," the old man explained,
"for this particular one has lately been experimenting with a
strange new form of gas, called nitrous oxide, which is, to all
reports, quite successful in eliminating such discomfort."

Rimbaud nodded to that, though, as things were, he was
rather looking forward to an experience which involved the
purging of one form of pain by means of another, even
greater, pain. By the time they had reached the office, how-
ever, and the old man had made payment and Arthur had
been seated in a chair not unlike that of a barber, he had
grown curious about this new gas, and asked the dentist if he
might inhale some as part of his treatment. The dentist, who
was fat, with a stale yellow beard, was delighted this young
man knew of his innovation, and he began to attach, some-
what clumsily, a black mask shaped like a cup over the poet's
mouth and nose. A long rubber tube ran from the mask to a
cylinder placed behind the chair. He turned a knob on the
mouth of the cylinder, readjusted the mask, patted the young
man's shoulder and told him to relax, that he would return in
a short time. "There is no time to speak of that is short," Ar-
thur was mumbling. "And there is a tiny German whose
clothing is in flames running in circles along the back of my
jaw." The dentist chortled and walked through the door to his
outer office; he knew the drug was already at work. The old

man had told him his young patient made claims to writing
poems, and now he would allow some time to pass before he
began extracting teeth, and he would let the poet dream.

So Rimbaud dreamt the nitrous dreams. Of women with
black skin whose lips were like drums. Of rodents sealed in
kegs of blue water. Of lightning shaped like freight trains
passing vertically through the branches of a tree. Whose
leaves were knives falling to the earth and standing upright.
There was a speed in these visions, each dissolved to the next
with thin wheels in flame dropping from the sky. And there
were words painted in many colors across the foreheads of
women whose arms linked like a chain. The smell of burning
rubber clung with thorny fingers to the ceiling of his skull.

Waking in a Painter's Loft in Paris

He woke and arranged the night's dreams across the floor like
playing cards. The flowers at bedside were strong with the
scent of valerian and scum. Feeling through his pants, draped
across the arm of a plain wood chair, searching for his pouch
of tobacco, Rimbaud felt the locket he had carried about for
years now in his hip pocket, presented to him by Izambard's
saintly aunts as he left them weeping at the staircase that last
visit . . . giving in to the demands of his mother's anguished
communication. He treasured the locket as he treasured these
sisters, not as the poet but as the youthful wanderer. Yet he
kept it concealed:

"I want my hands and neck to be free and clear," he had
told a school friend years before, "no crucifixes and no rings,
for my hands are decorated well enough by the coarse lines of
blood which run through them, sometimes forming vowels in
silver across my palms when the moon is right. . . ."

Rimbaud Running Guns

The representatives of the chieftain stride abreast through the
doors of the Great Bear Inn. The bronze stars inlaid across

their teeth caused men in corner booths to fumble for their notebooks. The seams of their robes brushed lightly across the sawdust. Their black skin could do nothing less than radiate the half-darkness of their surroundings . . . they knew no man in Marseilles wore upon his back a finer quality of silk.

Forming their words by the thrashing of the tongue against inflated jaws, they beat out the sounds:

"Rimbaud? We seek Rimbaud."

They sought in unison. They were four in number, one for each season, I would imagine, for the numbers of poetry would follow Jean-Arthur with the same intensity with which he sought to escape it.

"Speaking," summoned the poet, emptying a corncob pipe across the foot of a very fat man. He was with beard, now, less than a month . . . still, beneath it his skin remained the textured white of the gloves worn that day of first Communion. His eyes were his eyes only.

Rimbaud rose from a round table; playing cards tumbled from his sleeve. If it were the West, he would need to summon lightning from his hip. Here, in fact, painters with thick fingers laughed and coughed beer along the floorboards. The chieftain's main man, whom the others referred to as "Sire Ambassador," spoke in the same manner . . . that of a drum:

"We seek 43 gross rifle, the same, if you please, as the last; many, many bullets . . . whatever amount our bearers might safely transport; 16 Russian mortar launchers . . . or, as I suspect you prefer, a like number of American bazookas; and, finally, yet in the sacred eyes of our great Chieftain, most important of all these things, a Gatling gun."

"This shall be without difficulty," the poet replied. "I like the sound of that immensely, don't you?"

"What sound is that you refer, sir?" puzzled the black man.

"Gatling gun, dear Sire Ambassador," opined Jean-Arthur.

"Yes, it is quite lovely, this sound . . . it is not unlike 'Gathering grain' . . . no?"

Rimbaud Pays Homage to Saint Helena

His lips climbed the arc of Verlaine's back with such purity of
breath, he whistled "Ave Maria" against the thorny spine.
With this curling innocence revealed, he dared overturn the
master and fixed his eyes with pagan blessing on the gold
inlay of a crucifix chained to Verlaine's airy breast. He lent his
thumbs to a scarred nipple, caressing there with his need for
pain, and withdrew. He descended his lips and kissed the
feet of the jade Christ figure and fingered the cross with the
curiosity of a child inspecting gears beneath the skirt of a me-
chanical ballerina. Under the intensity of this tunneled scru-
tiny, Verlaine felt a sharp discomfort in his bowels. He
wanted to excuse himself to the end of the hallway but under
these eyes he was rightly pinned. It covered him without
warning and suffocated like a deadly pillow. Rimbaud turned
about the object with stained forefingers and undid a latch in
back of the cross with his fingernails, thin and dangerously
long.

It opened to reveal resting on a strip of liturgical velvet a
fragment of soft wood, the size of a starving insect. He sought
Verlaine's eyes:

"What, then, is this sliver of wood, which rests upon such
fine velvet?"

"It is a fragment of the true cross on which died the Savior
Jesus Christ, while wept beneath him a whore named Magda-
lene on the Mountain of the Skull."

Rimbaud had already known exactly what it was, and he
was amused by the prosaics of his companion's reply. He
knew also that this cross, with its gaudy filigree, must surely
be a gift from Verlaine's wife, whom he despised with a flow-
ing passion. Yet his eyes swelled, for the myth of his child-
hood was a breath away. They sank in that moment to his
lover's chest, where Verlaine could feel the quivering of lips.
Suddenly, like a piston, with a muffled speed, he drew up
with his teeth the sacred sliver from its antique bed, as a child
would remove a rose thorn from his fingertip. Verlaine bolted

straight up on the bed, the force knocked candles to the floorboards and hot wax sought the crevices. Already Jean-Arthur had leapt to the corner of the room, striking poses he had learned from bearded soldiers at the Commune barracks. And he swallowed the molding relic . . . and inhaled, deeply and seven times, the air available to him.

Verlaine leaned in disarray from the edge of the bed, his fists digging between tight thighs, the crucifix around his neck open. No question he did not notice the patch of velvet beneath him on the throw rug. His tongue locked by his teeth for silence. Rimbaud spoke:

"Now the history of Christ's death rests in my body, and will pass through by morning! Tell me, what poison could be more exquisite?"

Confederate Lake

She leans toward the left, her long hair in the oval mirror a
cameo that crawls. She thinks someone's watching; she won-
ders who she will be tonight. The brush in her hand combs
her thigh as her eyes grow large, and she hears a breeze
through the far trees, through their last leaves.

A taste, slow and dry, of fear winds itself between her
teeth, flawed by gaps, and settles casually beneath her
tongue.

The brush lands silent on the rug as the hand freezes,
opened and low. And the reflection turns to clear blue air be-
fore the mist rolls through. A breeze builds inside her ears.
She hears the sound of a tree falling on the still water of a
lake. She wonders which lake. She feels a sudden panic,
afraid it was Confederate Lake. Along Confederate Lake
there was only a single tree. It was huge and older than her
oldest relative . . . even those ones she barely remembered,
who were now dead. She thought of this lake as some others
remember a dog, or cat. It served her childhood summers.
The thickest branch reached from the sloped shore directly
out over the water, the clean water of innocence and clear
memory. From this branch her uncle had hung a hairy,
braided rope. They swung from the slope with a running
start, swallowing deep the danger of such still summer air.
Out they flew to the peak, more and more breathless, hanging
then in that moment of timelessness. They let go; the water
climbed toward them. They would stay late every day, until
the water turned cold for evening and they wrapped them-
selves in blankets between jumps, their teeth clicking in uni-
son. Killing time by picking the shells of cicadas from the
huge trunk . . . much like the shell she left in the mirror
now, as she walked hurriedly through the door to use the tele-
phone in the next room.

One Hundred Years of Boredom

There is a strange glow in the newborn's eyes, and the lips, though soft, seem the shade and texture of poached salmon. They smile and sneer, shifting sides in a single bent gesture. I think of the monoliths of Easter Island. The child turns its gaze on me as if it was not pleased with the looseness of connections within my thought. Surely I am exaggerating matters to myself . . . but now a few more new mothers enter the house to wish my sister well, united by the shrewdness of their fertility. The phone is not working. You probably knew that as well as I.

At least the road is sealed by the junta's men. It's the first thing they've done in years that I fully agree with. But I suddenly remember that the mail boat will be due to enter the harbor within an hour. I round up some couples from their siesta embrace and lead them to the water. There we set off the entrance to the harbor, with one long line of cheap barrels as a blockade, strung together by all the rope we could salvage from the general store. Looking down at it from the cliff now, it resembles the giant rosary of a simple monk. Surely this is a good sign. We are a simple people; we trust in God. And may we always have the faith to do so!

Silent Money

Long a diplomat of an illusion in decay, a devotee of a mimicry without source, he curls up lazily on the corner, like the tongue of a cat, and rails at each passerby with non-sequiturs, his hand extended only enough to make it difficult to reach. He likes the tentative shuffle.

He's sold every face he owns, and their shadows. Sometimes he bargains, "I'll die for your sins, if you will live for mine."

Yesterday, he arrived earlier than usual to find an ecologist with a stained beard in his spot. The man was bent over in a consumptive cough, holding a sandwich board which said, NOW OUR EARTH IS SHAPED / IN THE CHARACTER OF MAN. He didn't get what it meant. He screamed at him and threatened him if he didn't leave his area at once: ". . . or I'll kick your ass to the magic mountain." He was not dumb. In a past he barely recalled, he had read many books.

Sometimes, though rarely, he would engage me in a lucid conversation, letting loose the character he played. I remember in particular a dream he described. "I was right here, as I am in all my dreams (which I find horrible), and a woman . . . an old, bothersome woman, like the ones with the rags, shopping bags and lime-green shoes . . . asks me the time. I scream at her to go away . . . I mean, doesn't she see I have no watch? And the clock on the left spire of the office building across the square is broken. It *did* work once, you know . . . when did you first come around? Forget it. Listen. I'm screaming, and suddenly I am vomiting the hands of a clock . . . one about the size of a, say, kitchen clock, though they were in roman numerals, the numbers that followed the hands . . . and they were coated with that uranium stuff, like the wristwatches that glow in the dark. And the woman waits until it's all up and says, 'That's because you have eaten so much time.' Dumb shit dream, huh? I thought that was a good last line though, didn't you? Maybe you could write about it. It probably wouldn't be as good written down though. At least, that's been my experience. Oh, yes, *I've* tried writing myself . . . why do you think I always dream about this place. Always. I could be dreaming now."

What was strange about what he said was the part about me writing it down, since I'm certain I never told him I was a writer. He assumed other things correctly as well. It was that intuition of a beggar. Lazy as he was, he had the touch that was needed.

And that included knowing when a place was stripped barren. He left two days ago. All he said was he was trying, "Another cosmopolitan area." The spare change was getting sparse. It was all coin . . . thin coin. "A beggar hates loud money," he always said. "There is no sound as pretty as the sound of silent money."

Scouting

It's spring training for the major league ball clubs. Some people think I'm a big deal, working as I do for the big city team, but the fact is I'm small-time. I hang around the sandlots and playgrounds, which seem fewer and fewer each year as the cities themselves shrink, looking for a "viable commodity," as they are called in this new age. "Good prospect" was a term that used to suffice. The colleges, once a wasteland for real talent, are now the only consistent source of prime commodities. It's true, I do, even these days, find some kid who turns out to be the real thing . . . some kid with a cheap glove, a uniform whose top mismatches its bottom, on some playing field in the Bronx, with grass unmowed for three seasons, and basepaths of broken bottles of domestic beer. I try not to live in the past, but I can't deny the system was better in those days. The playing fields more charged with that strange energy of cool ambition and recklessness. Yes, it is more of a thrill to find a future star among the rubble, miles away from the flawlessly groomed diamonds of the campuses out west, where the uniforms fit as tight and suggestively as the leather and denim of a country singer . . . to reach back into the past and find that kid whose talent transcends all odds, even the whims of nostalgia I tie onto him, and watch him make it all real. It's true I get very little for my discoveries. The club throws me a bonus, which translates, if my pig Latin is correct, into being tossed a bone. *Bone* being *bonus*, the plural being *boni*. Indulge me this whimsy. I am old, and age breeds digression. Besides, with the money comes, each spring as now, a ticket by air to this place in the sun, where the young players treat me with a respect I am hardly worthy of, and even the oldest of the great veterans find time to come into the stands where I sit, and shake my hand and ask about the well-being of myself and my family.

Five Irresponsible Students of Zen

Five irresponsible zen students sit at the thick wood table for dinner. They are all related, and each is devoted to poetry. When they speak of zen, they are all in agreement. This is pleasant and understandable, for they each share the same teacher, and they believe him the greatest master in the city. When they speak of poetry, however, great disputes often arise, as each is devoted to the works of a different master. Their own poetry is mediocre. As students of zen, they are brilliant, though, as I have noted, quite irresponsible. Each has found what their teacher calls "the perverse hole" within their own deep powers of meditation. The master has noticed this with alarm, and, on more than one occasion, has warned the brothers of its dangers. He has warned them individually and, just that afternoon, gathered them together after the lesson and, again, reproached their method. They were laughing about just this as they sat at table, awaiting food.

Their mother, who is really their aunt, old and charmingly bent, serves them the special meal she has prepared: steamed rice cakes, shark tongue, and peacock eyes. There is much rice wine. They are celebrating the end of their formal training. Not used to the effects of saki, and having each toasted their teacher, they are soon quite drunk.

Thoughtlessly, they *become* the table. The room is quiet for a moment, then they release themselves. They laugh, spilling food from their mouths. They shake their heads violently, as if they had just emerged from a long time underwater.

Each quotes a haiku to honor the day, and another to pay homage to their teacher. They address their poem to an empty place set for their master. This is not formal tradition, but simply a drunken notion arrived at a moment before. Then, with a flawless lack of aim, they each balance a peacock eye on the tip of the chopstick. Held up to the last vestiges of day's light, the eyes are an iridescent blue and green. "Why, it is like the ring that converges in the center of the peacock's own feathers!" one notes. The others grunt. They are growing dizzy and numb. The peacock eyes spill off the sticks and roll across the mat. A cat appears from the garden and swats one savagely with its paw.

They decide to *become* the table again, and *become* the meal that lies, finished, across the table. Again, in their meditation, the sound of water rushing. But now the saki misleads their focus and the water's current grows . . . a knot in the table left by a worm . . . a ravaging whirlpool. The taste is salty, not sweet like a still pond. From the kitchen the aunt, a different aunt, hears a violent knocking of wood. As she enters the empty room, the cat bolts into the garden. She lifts the bowls as she calls out their names.

The Buddha Reveals Himself

That day when the Buddha first spoke at the deer park at Varanese some unknown merchant died in the exact place where, earlier that morning, a herdsman—who also was unidentified, though a younger man than the merchant—had died. Both died by the same means, drowning, within the same current, near an anvil-shaped rock some one hundred fifty yards off the banks of the River Indus, crossing on a raft secured by faulty knots (though neither raft was, as some had first suspected, the work of the same craftsman).

There was, apparently, a single difference between these tragedies. The herdsman left a legacy; the merchant did not. The herdsman's pig, it seems, was somehow rescued to the shore. The merchant's silver and jade, however, sank immediately to the dank, swirling bottom.

Me, Myself, and I

I was born in a pool. They made my mother stand. Gravity
was unsure of me from the start; as I slipped from the womb I
did not fall, but rose into the sky and over the cities. It was
night, and the clouds were restless. I have been this way ever
since. When I finally came down . . . when I was released
after days, no one left their buildings for weeks. I sought out
the streets near the filthiest markets for food, and their pure
silence was embedded in me. With the first sound of foot-
steps, I took to hiding behind the side altars of churches. I
worshiped there . . . not for God, but for silence. It was gone;
its pureness broken by the shifting of beads, a candle lit
loudly by arthritic fingers. I moved always down deeper, into
the storerooms beneath cold marble floors. In the darkness I
am the holiest of men. When I sleep, I am awakened by
blood from the feet of statues dripping across my eyes.

I am never bored. I entertain myself. I put deadly spiders
along my thigh, and they inject me with God. At times, I pre-
tend I am a man in order to laugh.

Past midnight, when the doors have been barricaded for
night, I ascend and steal water from the baptismal fount to
drink. For nourishment, I eat what moves across the floor in
the darkness. I have never seen my food.

What need have I for companionship? Without trying, I
have made an alliance with angels: my will and capability are
one. And, against my will at first, I was given comrades in
Hell. It is why I dance.

The saints know who I am. Because I dance, they have
made clear that they may offer me no aid. Yet, they have
vowed their respect for me nonetheless.

At night, to keep my body well, I climb these church walls
within. For footholds I use the reliefs of Christ on his way to
Calvary, as he weeps into a veil. Sometimes, as a great feast
day approaches, workmen use scaffolds to polish the facades.
They ascend all the way to the rotunda ceiling. It is my only
sky. I choke on the dead reliquary air of a hundred years. I
will be here on this scaffold, like an owl, for a hundred more.
Looking down, it is again the day of my birth. And I kiss the
painted blue. I touch the painted stars.

Teeth Marks

Tonight, in a codeine dream, I watched my father meet his own edges. He and my mother were standing in the kitchen doorway, beneath a vine of plastic grapes which my father had brought home seven years ago from the bar he tends. It had not been touched by any device for cleaning in all those years; there was a thin yellowed layer of dust covering the light green "fruit." Some benign blue light reflected off the linoleum floor and up their bare, painfully white legs. It accented the varicose veins across my father's calves; it reminded me of the display of sailor's knots in my Boy Scout Manual. I studied them years ago, and after being tested I would receive a small emblem, shaped like a wolf's paw, to sew across the pocket of my uniform. I was watching them from the living room floor, looking upward through my brother's legs. He was fat, and eighteen years of age. I was consistently thin with a thyroid condition, and two years younger. When the first raised voice was heard, my brother made for his drum in the corner. He slung it over his back and took the emergency stairwell up to the roof, where he had some masks out drying along the clotheslines. I heard my name and moved closer.

It was coming down. My mother was castigating him for some teeth marks forming crooked half-ass crosses on his nape. His vices were ever increasing, she was going on; he was pissing away my brother's crack at Harvard Law on the cockfights. She was bitching, as well, about him tapping too often into the goods down at the old tavern. He was half-loaded now, in fact . . . I could always tell by the greenish blotches of bile beneath his collar. She then made some reference, in sharply hushed tones, to his "putting the spiders to his jugular" with ever-increasing frequency. I didn't know exactly what she meant; she was pointing to three small punctures on the side of his neck, caked with dried blood, more blue than red in color. I thought back for a moment. I did recall one time catching him off guard in the bathroom tapping the sides of a small metal box with carrying handle and holes on the side, like the kind Oriental women use to transport their prize crickets. He was whispering some words I could not understand. I was about seven years old; he yelled at me for not knocking before entering a room and hastily shoved the box and whatever was in it out the window, where I heard it smash five flights below. He then wrapped himself in his largest fur and notified me he was going to get some fresh air. I looked in the alley beneath the window the next morning before going to school. I found nothing . . . I remember the old Irish woman who lived on the ground floor watching me from behind her window curtain with a look of horror on her face.

Reaching France

When I reach France, every promise will be kept. I want to be there, nodding in a chair from some bygone court in the hotel lobbies, with its back so high and its velvet arms. I'll sit beneath the sweet chandeliers and reflect my dreams off them, and they'll give it all back. Across the cathedrals of Paris the sun is bending, weary like the eyes of their marble saints, who blow cracked trumpets to the water birds at dawn.

I dropped out of school for sounds like that. I left it to those whose senses took the borders for granted. Who let their eyes be covered with the dull loose tissue of their dying fathers. Whose hearts did not make vows that marked those veins above my wrists for a lifetime. Left me here to pay the price which is a thin red poison that does nothing but lower the odds for my shot at love eternal. But keep your eye on me now, because I'll break each vow open, like a book that has lied to me . . . I'll leave it back where I found it in the streets for some other clever white boy to carry away.

Then I will never love these gifted whores again. Or think twice to stop and watch down a long corridor two old couples dancing slowly before dawn without once changing the music. I'll have enough money to confuse myself and I'll clutter my desk and rooms with empty boxes, and my lover's neck with jewels that whisper. Our children will come to us one evening near some ocean, with no regrets.

For now I lift up time at its edges and divide the day into quarters. When I am alone in this chair, I feel them dissolve like the darkness in a room before I take my aim. There are women with glasses and neat pleated skirts in a single row along the wall passing a baby through each other's arms. There are voices that aid me like a father, comfort me like a sister. Until the light shifts, and they crawl back to that dim alcove . . . saviors left unrecognized by heaven and its pedantic systems. Dressed neatly, with hair combed back straight. Do you know them? Do you know the place where I saw them last? Where the words have finally waited, and light in their eyes. And it's not France.

In the Law Library

I am sitting in the thin red glow of a library filled with texts on the law. The students have glasses to their lips. A tall black woman in a gospel gown is moving through the crowd with a silver tray extended before her. The tray is empty . . . yet, each student stops her, demanding more. In unison they turn to the mirrors lining the walls; their dull, loose skin turns cold and slides to their feet like silk scarves. On a revolving platform in the center of the room, one is standing describing the hardships of his youth. But he is over that now, he claims, and ready to ream any solid offer. He exposes his cock, and it is quite big. On it is the tattoo of a vault. But in the mirror it gives off no reflection. My sister is alone in the corner. She ignores the walls and uses the boy on the platform as a mirror. There she assembles her various parts. But she is sad. The last image has begun to fade. And there are no changes left.

There are few windows, and each of them is sealed. Outside, the sounds that hold morning with the wind are blue across the ice. A single bird is waiting along the line, like a small block of darkness left behind by night. Inside, some workmen are rushing to cover the windows with more mirrors. They face other mirrors. The mirrors are full. The bird is gone.

In the Capital

I come from another age, and in my dreams I meet with presidents and their daughters on my own terms. What do they make of the nearness of my features? The father seems more tired than most, dead blood hanging beneath his eyes like rotting grapes. On his index finger is a green ring that gives off signals. With a wave of his hand he commands the air, and it responds by blowing back his daughter's long dark hair for passing photographers. She's got something in a tweed shoulder bag, and it won't stay still. She whispers to me and I walk away, then I come back with much more than before and take her down. The lawn is wet and glistening black in places like perfect onyx. She tells me it is the dried black semen of the general from Chile who had visited last week. "He met with my father over lunch and talked about some shipments," she said. "Then he went off and blew up his ambassador and a grey limo . . . and that's no dream, motherfucker." I liked her. When I came, I went. I watched her father growing smaller as he waved from behind a gate.

In the fracture of dawn in the capital of Washington, I gather ticks from the ears of patient dogs on the steps of the Supreme Court. It is raining a deep rain, it blocks the morning light as it tries to enter. I see women rush by with bracelets around their ankles with pearls the size of golf balls. They smile at me. What do they make of the nearness of my features? One has snagged her anklet on a hydrant, and the pearls are scattered across the sidewalk. I'm sitting on the steps of some tomblike memorial to a man I have never heard of. I take one of the pearls up with my boots and roll it back and forth between my legs against the cool, fine marble. A woman whose ankles are bare takes my wrist lightly and leads me inside the memorial, past columns of steel painted black. Beneath an unkempt glass rotunda there is a statue, half man-half fish. The woman leans her tongue to my ear: "It is strange, but that is natural . . . the sculptor was a man who left behind nothing with his death but this fractured memory from a mind which was very mediocre and very overpaid. We are, after all, 'in the capital.' "

Stepping Out of M.O.M.A.

I was a blonde along Fifty-third Street with a red bandanna pulled tight to hold back my hair. I wanted to be pure. Women from another class approach me with their dresses raised to prove to me the sheerness of their stockings. They smile. They do not smile because they are happy; they smile because they are clever. In the late afternoon, at 5:15 p.m., people left the massive glass office buildings and the bells began. It happens each day. I want to know them all, I want to come to understand them, but not one face leaves a clue. Only those who want me reveal themselves, so I must make myself wanted by each. Those who pass by too quickly for my eyes to reach, I follow. I trail them to the steps of the subway station across from the loading platform and ask if I may borrow their diary for the night.

I know this city will die before the fall of evening. I lean against a slick cool marble cornerstone with my shirt undone and my blue eyes sinking like wet lips down the shoulders of women. It is what I do each day, though I know neither they nor I will be doing it tomorrow. The others knew it as well . . . women in thin shrouds fingered rosaries and mumbled vague chants of purification. Construction workers in steel hats formed lines from confessionals to street corners. Still, they deny me my last access. I throw aside my bandanna and let my hair roll across the lips of women who have prostrated themselves to the hollow flux. Out of bitterness I walk down to the cathedral.

I was pure, sitting along the steps. Then, with the changing of wind and music, I stood and watched its shadows take the horizon. I knew what this was and what it meant, but I could not make it to the drugstore in time. With the white heat, I dropped across the fender of a halted limousine. Some tried to outrun their screams, the smart ones went down. And, right beside me, I noticed the mother of a girl I had once loved so badly. She wore a string of pearls around her neck, and, noticing me, she smiled . . . she tore apart the necklace and poured the pearls down my throat and her own. I felt pure; I placed my swollen tongue to her lips. Neither of us had come this far to die with strangers.

Days

I.

I meet my sister just before dawn beneath a pale statue on Columbus Circle and we take the "A" train uptown to its last stop. It is always cold and drizzling slightly at the end of each and every subway line of New York City. There are processions passing of old Irish women returning from night with shopping carts on small wheels, filled with lye wrapped in damp newspapers. Their coats are too thin for winter and split at the edges as they pull across the sidewalks like flags dragged back from some battle lost. They chant indolently to the leaving of darkness, then scatter into any doorway as the sun breaks its first lines over the great wall where two rivers meet. We have coffee in a restaurant filled with Greek workers, walk two blocks and turn through a doorway, drink a vial of codeine solution each before ascending five flights in the dark elevator. We were born in this building . . . and raised. Rising, we hear the sound of waves crashing against the elevator doors and ceiling.

We visit our mother four times a year, always on the same days . . . as if to delineate clearly for her the passing seasons. We enter with our keys rather than ringing the bell. Her legs are crippled . . . they no longer work . . . and she is bound to bed. A nurse comes each day but she has not yet arrived. That is our purpose in coming so early. She is awake as we enter her room, which was once ours, sitting up in bed reading through the instructions to a stained glass hobby kit she had received last week in the mail.

The bed our mother lay in was constructed on her own orders. It rose so high off the bedroom floor that my sister, who is nearly six feet tall, barely had to bend over as she kissed the old woman's powdered cheeks. There was a small stepladder within reach to one side, and both sides were secured, a few inches above the mattress, with two steel bars. "It is in case of another seizure," she explained, anticipating a question we probably would not have asked anyway. "After the last one I lay cringing along the floor with both wrists absolutely shattered for close to six hours before that damn spic nurse arrived and dragged me back up. Can you imagine, they sent me a Puerto Rican girl? It wasn't even one of the light-skinned ones. That was from that first agency, the one that you hired, Meg," she spoke, glaring at my sister, "I never thought I'd be thrown from some claptrap bed when I was young and rode to first place in the summer rodeo near your great-grandmother's swamp house in South Jersey . . . do you know I dream of those rodeos more than any other time of my youth? That says a lot, you know, for there were so many splendid things I did in those years. I was a beauty, like you, Meg . . . One summer, the year before your father and I were married, I believe it was, I was named Miss Greenwood Lake. It was a real resort back then too . . . not that acre of piss it was last time I saw it, where college kids go to get drunk—puking, no-class drunk, I mean—over the Easter break. You still have that picture of me with my hair down to the waist, don't you, my son? The one where you said I looked like Saint Veronica? Wasn't she the one that wiped the sweat from the face of Christ on his way to the mountain of the skull to die, leaving his image on her veil? That Puerto Rican nurse would know which one she was. She swore she was a regular reference catalog on saints!" I nodded back to her as she closed her eyes to sleep . . . yes, I think that's who Veronica was, though I never remember comparing her to that ancient photo of the old woman on the bed before me. Yet, she was beautiful and, yes, I still have the photograph some-where in the green album at home.

Our mother was deep asleep now, exhausted by the words spoken on her youth. Her head was raised up by seven varie-gated pillows, the top one covered by a satin case, the others with some cheap fabric, each of them with the name of a New Jersey resort motel labeled in the corner. I thought she looked sort of strained in the neck this way, so I slipped five of the pillows out from the bottom of the stack. She opened her eyes a second, said nothing, and fell back off to sleep. There was a cat dozing as well on the mattress directly beside her head, his tail resting across her throat. The cat was twenty-three years old. He was so fat, he looked more like an owl. For the past four years, I had never once seen him with his eyes opened. From the day I brought him home from the cellar of the old apartment on Seventeenth Street, he knew he had found a home. Now he refused to let go. Somehow he continues to breathe. I spoke to him once; he had nothing to say.

My sister and I looked into each other's eyes. She took my hand in hers and raised it to her parted lips and began to circle the crevice of each finger slowly with her tongue. When she stopped a moment, breathing deep, I followed her eyes to a picture on the wall above the bedboard. It was the two of us, ages fourteen and twelve. "God, we looked more alike than we do now," she whispered, "we wasted a lot of time back then in the room we shared together." I pulled down her hand and led her out the door of our mother's room. "Let's go see how that room looks now that we're smarter about things like time."

The room had not changed much. When we woke, I wiped something from her bottom lip and searched my own with my tongue. "From the way the day is going," she spoke, a little too loud for the moment, "you would think it was no different than any other time we came to visit her." And we both knew she was right. We hurried getting ourselves ready and back to the other bedroom. Mother was still asleep, the cat had not moved its tail. I took up one of the pillows I had removed earlier. In the corner in thin red script it read, "Bermuda Palms Motel, Atlantic Beach, N.J." I turned around the cat so that its owlish cheek lay aside my mother's. I lowered the pillow to the place and pressed down, softly, yet tight enough so that the veins on my forearm rose as if summoned by the needle. As I held it there I looked up toward my sister. Her lips were half parted and her eyes stared at the picture above the bedboard. "You know, Christmas isn't that far off," she muttered. "That photo would have made a wonderful card to send our friends."

159

II.

We took a cab straight to the airport; sister didn't move her
head from my shoulder all the way to San Francisco. The lim-
ousine we had called ahead for was there in line behind two
others. We could tell it was ours by the cross within the circle
painted on the side. The back seat was purple velvet, the
floor covered with eucalyptus leaves. As we moved along the
freeway with the wind through the open window the scent
carried us back to when we were young, home from school
with colds in winter after weekends riding down hills near our
cousins' home in New Jersey on pieces of linoleum after some
bigger boys had taken away our sleds. Our aunt would rub
some medicine, warmed with boiling water, across our chests.
The leaves on the floor of the big black Cadillac now smelled
the same as that rub. I reached down my sister's blouse and
cupped my hand, with its palm filled with spit and crushed
eucalyptus, over her breast. She turned her eyes and smiled.
"I remember," she said.

The driver made a turn off the freeway a few minutes after
we had crossed the Golden Gate, heading for the ocean. The
driver was a black woman, nearly six feet tall. She was
eager to please, the cross within the circle painted on her
sharp cheekbones was fading from the day's heat as she
turned her head to inform us how much time was left. "Have
they cleared off the beach?" I inquired. She told us that they
had. She formed her words by bouncing her tongue off the
roof of her mouth and the hollow of her cheeks, like a ball,
and each syllable was clear and precise. Not only did she say
what we had wanted to hear, she seemed to say it in exactly
the manner we wanted to hear it as well. "She's delightful,"
my sister whispered, "I knew mother was wrong about that
agency."

I had never driven on a road like this one. There were
many curves, and around each some jelly-fish substance
seemed to move up and down along the two yellow lines di-
viding the lanes. In the opposite lane, leading back to the

city, the chant continued from the speakers assembled across the platforms of large, speeding trucks. At last we reached the base of the mountain's far end. The driver rolled casually through the streets of a small oceanfront town. Darkness was just settling over the firehouse. It was the tallest building in sight, and the siren-shaped speaker on the roof played on the deep chant. Some workers in tight wool trousers were returning home from the chapel near the redwood grove, their wives trailed with sickly infants straddled around their necks. Prayer beads, the size of cranberries, were fastened to their belts with plain wooden clothespins. The driver turned to us and spoke, "These are a very independent people, we offered much money to keep them off the streets this evening but it is *novena* time and they would not listen . . . the beach, however, will be cleared as promised . . . we are nearing it now, in fact . . . this would be a good time for you to sign the register." She held before us with her long fingers a large book, bound with barblike wire and covered in suede. A pen inside marked the place for my sister and myself to sign. We then turned the page and, in the blank space following, added the proper remarks. The car engine stopped. We sat at the top of a twenty-five-foot ramp, leading directly to an empty beach below. The Pacific Ocean was at high tide, so that the waves swept a full five feet beyond the base of the ramp. I looked at my sister. She held out her hand for mine.

The driver stepped outside and spoke to a genteel old man with soft grey hair. He was dressed in a tweed three-piece suit and, at one point, laughed casually at a remark the tall black woman had made. The meeting lasted only a few moments; she handed him the suede-bound register and returned to her seat behind the wheel. She said nothing more. Two young women in plain tan skirts and no top clothing to cover their large breasts opened the doors beside my sister and me and proceeded to bind our hands with silk stems and place thick strips of fur across our eyes. They asked about our comfort and withdrew. We could hear the gravel move under their feet and the sound of a car door slammed shut as they began a conversation on the beauty of the light across the upper ridges of the mountain at this time of evening. The driver began the engine. I could feel my sister's breath leaning closer to my ear: "We have waited too long before moving into eternity." We felt the car plunge forward.

As we heard the waves plunge through the four open windows, the fur was released from our eyes, the stems were freed from our wrists. We watched the driver dissolve behind the wheel like a mannequin in a pool of acid . . . only her two eyes remained, shaped like glass almonds; they rose with the clear green water to the roof of the car and set there, frozen, fixed down on us with an ominous detachment. I took my sister's hand, now I would never let it go. We would glide forever. She smiled. Her eyes filled with a surfaceless light. I tried to lead her by the hand out the window. We could glide.

But I was wrong. The desires inside our dreams are not fulfilled therein. I saw in her eyes she too had realized it, just before the crosscurrent swept in. It slashed my fingers in hers, cold and quick like a frozen knife. She was being pulled away, out the window and at my left. The fast water pushed my screams back into my lungs, I was being pulled away . . . in another direction. Always and forever, in another direction. . . . I wanted to let go, but somehow I continued to breathe.

And each dream is of distance. I move like a shark, never sleeping and never ending, and always an equal three feet and no more from the milky azure floor. I touch nothing, and nothing will touch me. My speed is always the same. It is neither fast nor slow. It is the speed of some aging thief, stolen himself by the tide. I hear constantly a chant of unyielding distance. I do not age. My eyes pump upward some strange dull light. What I speak is pressed back inside before the words are formed, so there is no longer a language by which I can think. The only thought is distance.

And it is the same for her. The same speed, the same distance from the ocean floor, the same thought, the same dream. She circles the earth in another direction. And once a year we pass each other, on that date that marks our act together. Even for that moment the dream does not change, of distance. And we do not touch, although our hands are forever extended. Even the light pumped upward from our eyes does not meet; it runs parallel, instead, to the surface, raised by distance into the sky.

The Transient

They were the cheap rooms on that floor, with the bathrooms
down the hall. Late at night, through his insomnia, he
counted the times the women used their shared toilet, espe-
cially the giggly pair in the room two doors down. They were
young; they'd been there only two days. One always seemed
to take an awfully long time, much too long to simply urinate,
even taking into account, as he did, the possibility that they
were drinking California wine throughout the night. "She is
maturbating; it is obvious." He said this, for some reason, out
loud, and realizing what he had done, realizing that he might
easily be overheard by one of the passing women, he wrote
out a note on yellow paper. It said, in block letters, "Talk
silently to yourself," and he attached it with some tape to the
frame of the mirror. He returned to the image he held of her
(it seemed unbalanced . . . tentative and precarious). This
time he kept silent, however. Maybe that was why it slid
back and forth. She was rubbing her clitoris in circles with the
tips of her pinky and thumb pressed together. She was cooing
very softly. Again, he mimicked this imagined sound, ab-
ruptly, a sort of glottal strut, out loud, then quickly checked
himself, peering up to the mirror and shaking his head . . .
these things were difficult. Lacking any imagination, she
thought of nothing in particular as she manipulated her-
self . . . only of the narcissistic pink color of the door before
her. (He knew the color, having used the ladies' room himself
when no one was around.) The expanse of pink opened out
in her mind to a meadow of blinding pink light, pink as the
clitoris she now rubbed (her fingers pressed together in a
triangle, like some oriental greeting).

He always used the more clinical choice of words in his
inner dialogues, like "clitoris" or "penis" . . . never resorting
to those vulgar euphemisms. He thought words used in their
formality were much sexier. He heard these words spoken al-
ways in a voice not quite his own . . . an assured, command-
ing female voice . . . that of a wealthy child's guardian, or,
more specifically, the voice of that one woman doctor on the
staff of the ward he had occupied those three Christmases

ago, the doctor he always asked to have his sessions with, but was never allowed, forced to see the Chinaman instead.

She was returned now to her room, her roommate having answered the squirrel-like knock, and they were giggling again as if she had never left. "God, the doors here are thin," he thought, "can they hear me when I sing along with the radio?" He panicked at this notion. Resolved NEVER to do THAT again, never to sing out loud. He drew another piece of stationery from the drawer and wrote out a reminder which he again taped to the mirror, this time to the bottom of the frame. It read, "Thin door . . . don't sing either . . . ever . . . but inside is O.K."

He heard the girls' voices louder now. He didn't mind that. He enjoyed hearing them, though he wondered what there was to laugh about constantly. Then he thought . . . no, he was certain . . . that he could distinctly hear a man's voice among the two girls'. Suddenly their giggling annoyed him incredibly. He felt it as a physical force, like a branch snapped in his face by some wholly inconsiderate stranger passing before him, single-file, through a thin trail in a woods which he suddenly recalled. Like a cuffing across his frost-stung ears by a nun as he arrived late on a winter morning. The giggling no longer seemed airy and expansive, trailing out into nothing but the hallway. It seemed now stifling . . . tightly enclosed and claustrophobic, moving directly into his brain . . . into the small room which was *his*, which *he* had rented (at daily rates). Now all their silly, childish laughter was only in response to the deep voice of a male he pictured, obscenely between them, lying back on the single bed's spread with the same orange and brown pattern as his own.

He was surely dark, this fellow, his belt was unfastened and, apparently, he didn't care. His bass voice seemed to curl like a jungle trellis or snake around objects and tighten itself there. At this moment it was fastening itself around the girls' wrists. He was waiting, hoping, in fact, that they would scream for help, yet they only continued with their ridiculous giggling. He felt a swift anxiety and rage . . . the smooth

165

walls of his room were appearing to crack into wet stone blocks, as in a cell. He tried an anxiety-reducing breathing exercise which the black nurse on the midnight-to-eight shift had taught him. It involved breathing through alternate nostrils, but he couldn't remember which nostril to begin with and that, as he recalled, was all-important. The walls were dripping . . . he tried beginning with the left nostril. It seemed to work. The walls began to look smooth again. He felt the plaster. It was smooth . . . nice.

He was about to call the desk to complain, but he thought better of it. He was mindful of another nurse he favored back there telling him that they had great difficulty placing him in this hotel, and not to cause any trouble . . . to be as inconspicuous as possible. He jumped up and made another, smaller sign in block letters, taping it beside the others on the mirror. It read, "Be inconspicuous."

Already standing, he headed to the washbasin. He preferred that term to the word "sink," it was listed that way in the hotel's brochure which they had sent him: SINGLE ROOMS, INCLUDES WASHBASIN, ADEQUATE BATHROOM, BATHING, AND SHOWER FACILITIES IN HALL (he liked the word "facility"). He began to run the hot water. It was very hot; he could brew tea in the morning or prepare instant coffee with water run hard, directly from the tap. The rising heat fogged up the mirror of the medicine cabinet above the basin. Then, as if to prove a natural, God-given advantage over the giggling girls who, by a necessity to squat, need use the toilet down the hall, he proceeded to piss directly into the flow of water, watching a spiral jetty of wax-thin yellow circle the drain and disappear . . . the steam forming droplets on his penis. When he was through, zippering back up his pants, he looked up into the mirror. In the fog formed in the glass there from the vapors' ascent he, without realizing or intending to (so that it somewhat shocked him), had written plainly, "Have found the only advantage of being a man."

Just Visiting

When the shooting broke, I decided to vault the teller's window and face the fire from the other side. They saw my forearm tightening across the throat of the cashier, Ms. Lattimore, and as my Browning was raised to her temple's pulse, they took it back. It all fell dead; with the silence I felt the distance between my trigger and the man. I heard the reverberation of the last stray bullet's muffled ring; it moved out through my brain in circles of jagged light expanding like still water broken by a stone. Some smart lieutenant arrived to take things over. He leaned his eyes a moment through the doors, then went around back to throw the switch. The light rolled out of thin vapor tubes above me from right to left. The darkness absorbed more silence. I could hear their details being assigned. The tone of the head man's voice was clear: they were hot to blow me away. I didn't expect my hostage would go down as a deal, I knew she signed *that* paper when she took the job . . . but I just wanted some last contact. I would have rather some sweet clever music. I slit the strap to her bra I reached under I felt my palm rinse her breast. It could have been a radio. I moved my lips closer so only she could hear me. It should have been a radio.

Whispering, I told her, "You see, all my life the women I have been with . . . and that's more than you could imagine, really . . . I always bypassed their breasts I went down, you know, I went to the source I honestly don't think you're going to die so don't be afraid, listen . . . I wanted the thunder on my fingers, on my lips. What are a woman's breasts? Just so much adornment . . . they lie like some chalice on an altar waiting for adoration. Like the writing on the scroll . . . the handles on the urn . . . the gold that lines the vessel. I wanted the mystery inside. The thunder and the darkest light. I mean, I feel the sharpness of your nipple, it is flawless, no doubt about that, just let me move it over here, oh, it came out . . . it's so red. You must be younger than you appear . . . I know about that kind of thing, really. Once I told

this girl she had breasts like bleeding lemons, she thought
that was a beautiful thing to say. But what are they? . . .
just architecture, where is the wetness? And why are they so
white, so terribly white? Whiteness frightens me horribly.
When I was fourteen years old, I went to my friend's house at
the beach in Long Island. The sun there on the sand, I re-
member it, it was terrible . . . too much whiteness. I couldn't
stand it I stayed in my friend's room for days and listened to
music. His mother and his fat sister thought me quite insane.
I wanted to teach myself to play the drums. The sister was
thirty-six years old and so fat, the mother had to tie the laces
of her shoes. I hated her and she hated me, but I was just
visiting so it wasn't very fair. One day I bolted out of the
bathroom while she was listening, leaning up to the door and
I jammed a pencil into her jaw. She ran away crying about
lead poisoning, but you know, you really can't get lead poi-
soning that way, it's a wives' tale. I know about these things,
really. At night, when the shadows cancelled the blinding
white, I'd go down to the beach and run because it is impor-
tant to keep the body well. That's in case they ever come
again. You, I'm sure, don't concern yourself much worrying
about them, do you? You know, your breasts are like that
beach, so white and dry . . . yet so near to the source . . .
the water and the motion of the waves . . . what could ever be
more pure? Please allow me to just feel down here . . .
I won't try to sneak anything up the wrong hole I know that
can hurt if you're not used to it. They did it to me. I let them
think I didn't really care but I found a closet down at the
end of the tier and I hid in it and learned things and made
marks on my forearm with a fork I snuck from the cafeteria.
You can see here, the scars. It's not just an X, it's actually an image
of the cross Saint Peter died on. They nailed him to it inverted,
he's my patron saint. Ahhh . . . there it is . . . and wet . . .
from fear? Wetness is not whiteness but so dark. Whiteness
is the color of death, you know, not black. Wetness

is life, the breeder and shaper of life. In the beginning the sun was black. So all light was absorbed before it had a chance to return. And our dreams, then, were empty."

New York City Variations

Noiselessly, the world has begun to defect.

New lampposts curve over the avenue
in darkness, like chrome tears.
In sunlight, drops of android sperm
frozen above traffic, loud and green. I live
on an island where I was raised, flanked
by rivers. To the east, great bridges.
To the west, tunnels. Palisades. Sunsets changed.

This bridge an old, sinking web,
the trapped scales of a saxophone
Struggling to set themselves free.
They will fall one day, sink small ships
passing beneath with the weight accumulated
over years. Carbon dioxide and ice. Crystals
from poisoned towers. Hats and veils from war
widows, crossing for Easter. 1949. 1951. Fragments
of hydrogen bombs, dark from the Pacific. Screams
from jumpers, released from Bellevue, like spiders, returning
the night I was born, to claim prey in midair.

The moss under your fingernails it feeds
on the sweat of my lips. I remember that.
It was summer the ships were towed back to port.
Uptown the yellow taxi pulled away leaving your hair
to dry in the wind. I have been living beneath the streets
under the sharp blue light of subway wheels. I know the
   streets above.

My training ended at twenty-three years of age.
There was nothing left but the mountain of the sacred
   maiden.
And you. You with weeping wrists and your chaste forehead.
who drove all night to meet the sun
in the eyes of ascending gulls, gulls who haunt my poems
like hands of apostles in the sky.

I have walked these streets so often I could
forge the shadows of skyscrapers as they fall
to rest below the sculptured air of midtown.

Air-conditioned blood drips like rosaries
from glassy facades to the cosmopolitan eyes

The fantasies of secretaries are washed to the streets
or trampled beneath thick heels along subway platforms.

Engineers in orange helmets point out the flawlessness
of buildings which do not yet exist. My hands

drain with boredom or lust. It was time
for evening in Times Square. There the dim-witted clouds
at once unbuttoned, revealing a nasty aperture beneath
    thin blue cables.

I stored daylight in secret attics
since I fell in love with guns,

my youth sealed in vaults crowded
with an infant's idea of Heaven.

Night rising straight and fatal as a vacant syringe.
Seven times it fell in blocks, immediate as a bloodstained
    image.

We had pride in our bodies . . . they moved
with the sureness of death across cathedral walls

Our coats hugged us slick as the sharkskin air
And in our jeans we dreamt of Times Square empty at dawn.

Concealing weapons, we crashed under boardwalks
near ocean's amusement park and in the sky its stars

blew some riffs lightly.

My body has been perforated
with a strange idleness. From it chaos
flows like blood trailing an abcess,
the poison itself long since passed.

Precision, I build this altar
to you. For what was taken
from me, I need

A competent God to praise,
to raise me above
new cities, whose climate
is grace. Still
gardens of winter. A bell.

Thick veins on the back of my forearm,
like the rope of an acrobat,
have risen again

As a line of demarcation
between fields of battle
which vacillate easily but with some small pain
across this flux of anguish between light and dark

past and future   ash and flowering flame.

What matter for thick armchairs and fine shelves for books?
I chose apartments for loose floorboards to hide the secret.

On Fifth Street the bell at the window summoned children to
    classes.
Toward night the sirens emerged. I mastered the raging of
    birds
Rising through floodlights. I collapsed across the black sheets
And ripped open my back on the fingers of dried sperm.

Voices from a red radio come down,
pin me to this bed as if many
iron bars were sealed against my wrists.

There is an owl outside this window.
It follows me through Manhattan, persistent as the blocks
of sunlight at dawn. And there are cities.

I was born and surrendered in the city
and it has made a difference . . .
when I hear the owl I think of stones.

It comes through the window
as if the balance might be restored.
And I sing because the long wait has ended
And raise the floorboards where under the sinking
of an eyelid like a blue vault sleeplessness sits with folded
    arms.

Here I walked with a memory of workers in midtown
returning at day's end to safe edges of home near water

Streets abandoned to a purer grace, until the summit
of tall buildings is where the light of evening sleeps

And in the slit shadow below, blasting my way
through the taxied vapor, I finger the turbine mist

I wait on the origin of night's sounds waking, I know
that here only the blind man sings, even in rain

The notes of drenched violins turn like warped mirrors
and the last cloud parts slowly, like a cracked wheel.

It seems I have misplaced the directions for childhood.
The maps laid across my veins are changed by sick night.

Outside the women form rings
that neither sing nor dance
but chant to an angel in white gloves
whose eyes speak fever and dissolution.

Yet in my room   Youth charts its distance.
The fragments of my rage descend   like a moth
from this ceiling to lie across the quilted evening
Smashed tentacles of inertia,   I am trying

To abide by rulings. The half-fulfilled dream aside,
I walk here dangerously across ice or stone
With nails in my boots like a lame stallion.
Dogs came to my hand and spit to seal
the punctures in my forearm and I am again
a part of the condition   of man
by the grace of their tongues.

Back to the streets always, ravaged and wet,
strained with midtown exhaustion, late afternoon
when the clever walkers funnel the wind of taxis
or shift to the sky to peel wet words from their eyelids.

The strangers with slick hair are wont
to strangle schoolgirls at these mirrored hours.
And the shadowed edges are worn and light is towed
by buses and the nod is shattered in the sheer height
of federal buildings further down. I watch this island
where I too was born and spent my youth walking, not
    waking.

Walking on grey on green in Central Park I wore
slit jeans and a shirt from Jamaica blue and yellow
with a hood and many red buttons I did not own it.

Some detectives in worn suits slide at my door.
They told me Eddie was dead on Lexington and 103

stabbed in the jugular at mid-day
outside two automated hospital doors.

He often walked East Harlem after dark, high
on reds, calling out the black man. Before the sheet
    descended

on his eyes he grabbed the nurse's wrist
to check the blood was real, he signed one last paper

to donate properly his eyes.

And I salute you, my brother.

My needs were few and pure.
I swept powder through the green shafts and sought
to understand the grace in death on subway toilets.

I took the time to lie
in barber chairs in lobbies of ruined hotels
and breathe antiseptics surrounded by mirrors.

I drowned my own eyes and surfaced
to jars of combs in varied sizes
like strips of human brain preserved for a woman of substance
who waits across the lobby on sofas of crushed red velvet
guarded by shadows bought by years without sunlight.

At eighteen years of age,
Sad on the ridge of Upper Manhattan
under the Cloisters' Spanish shadow
I wanted my blood to wash clean the Palisades.

I came close to binding myself within a stolen tapestry
to drop from the rail of the George Washington Bridge
and shatter against the drifting condoms
that float like dead eels across the Hudson by dawn.

In midtown again the way you stop
casually to finger your hair
in some grey drugstore window
across Fifty-third Street the Museum of Modern Art,
that poverty vault.

I fell right through the deep there once.
I felt the light of Nolde scratch beneath my fingernails
and I found poverty once more.

So much poverty. It follows me through subway cars.
Poverty to die a death within one's own family.
Poverty of the darkness across the ice. Poverty of cataract
      eyes.
Poverty of young men alone behind the stairway, who practice
alchemy inside bottle caps, who know
the altruism of a last syringe.

I watched a street gang heading
at me on East 106th, their hands
touched the pavement as they walked.

Tired of cheap revolvers and exploding fingers
they came to understand the beauty of the knife

And I ran. I clutched the twin scorpion in my crotch.
I was thirteen years of age I was pretty I was white.

Marked by a more distant sky, I hold
a black sponge to flush darkness
in the thin canals of night
between midtown buildings.

In this city.
In this century.

I squeeze it above my head
to rinse my eyes.
when I am tortured by women passing
more beautiful than the unnamed flowers
that bloom in the dreams of children
dying of fever.

In another century.
In another city.

Children more fluid than gardens
Unveiled in some future desert
beyond the shift
sleepless with thirst and memory
far from the city. The cities are dead.

A place more brillant than women,
or the scream of the earth's own sun. Or
dark, then, as this moment returns, a loneliness
which rests tonight, greets me at dawn
with its cruel, smashed fingers.

I drank cough syrup in alcoves
of vast men's rooms in Grand Central Station.
The eyes of broken commuters leaned
against me like tender knives.

And I took trains
to wealthy suburbs to walk their streets
and summon up clap from queenly town daughters.

I settled in Rye at midnight
walking until dawn, the tall reeds
near the cemetery were fingers
that beckoned me to lay.

And with the sun I set
on the graves of soldiers dead from the Revolution
and understood there the hilarity of fear.

Not surprisingly
I lost track of the seasons
writing biographies of the haunters
of my dreams in infected urine.

As if time had been mine
to blast anyone away
in the stare of my ambition.

Check the way
the gargoyled facades are dissolving
in the hot breath of tubercular doves
over Duffy Square when the sirens ring at noon.

Then Christmas on earth will burn in this city.
The furnished rooms, just down the street,
are filled with flaming white hair . . .

and I must go now and assume this responsibility.

When he was young in Harlem my father
watched the shadow of St. Anne, the mother
of Our Virgin, walking with shadowed gown
round a church rotunda, white as chalk and swept
with decals of starry blue why should I not believe him?

I cannot return. Never go back. Yet my father's word
has weight in its edges to stand straight like shields
and here I wait in the exhaust of his space and time
rolling my wrist with bandage to check the flow
of spit from the veins, the mucous music sticks
to fixtures on top these hotel dreams, parking lots
behind the Chelsea on West 22nd crowded with monolith
    lungs and dew
piles of dancing shoes . . . some guitar claws.

I rest with the dogs across the feathers of birds
    departed for winter.

I hear thinly colored dew forming beside me, eyes vacant
in the stupor of redwood fog . . .
sweat and shattered hair down my forehead
like boneless fingers of children back home.

Distant, alone without language or fear

as if I were among those wounded at war
left across an open courtyard
in a village far from Paris or Milan

hearing the small voices of women in love.

I am trying to abide by the clues
in the dreams left half-fulfilled,
on the deathbed of each brother,
where the tears of a sister stained the milk-white sheets.

And I look to my generation
and dream in blasts of hydrogen,

where the residue of all my nights
is changed to stars.

The process is a circle, is brilliant and works,
as the final collapse of dying suns cradles new ones to life.

Like a rabid goat, this obsession
runs crazed
Until the desire itself
is broken and wasted
beneath the weight of its hooves.

The torn clover leaks and slides
beneath it. Some greater flower
evolves from the strain.
The suffering relives its past.
The echo recedes to a former voice
and the canyons which carried it upward,
To passing birds, close in their walls.

On the cliff
I cover my dream
with fallen tents
that held them in sleep,
the sleep of pale quivering eyes,

the canvas marked by angry teeth
like the skin of seals. I carry them off,

bury them with precision or flames.

Poems 1973–1985

Poem
for Frank O'Hara

My footsteps in the shallow
Ocean pools, the poisoned lips
Of the anemones set loose my eyes
To fly to the horizon, time's own memory

I see a single ship passing,
Shadowless, that one which never
Arrived, as you stood, years before,
Waiting in the harbor, dressed for love,
Your loose breasts throbbing as if beneath
Their surface small fish were feeding on your heart.

Winter's Age

Your hands are like two mirrors which press
dry the flowers so many young daughters have
chosen for the blind and the grave.

Beneath halves of walnut shells
my eyes are switched, back and forth,
in the slight fingers of a confidence man.
So for all these years I have had to cheat to see.

The red and softly frozen sky
is transformed by night on these streets
To tears without faces. Without reason.

Where are the noble tears,
tears which, fallen, from thorns
beneath the rose, the tears which convert
the frail peasant girl to a saint of roses?

Remember this: The past draws blood.
Its fingernails are cut off
on the edges of old winter skies,
forgotten and forgiven. They fall, stiff and black
Like dead hornets into the soft treetops.

For Elizabeth

It is winter, ending on earth.
The planets align tomorrow
in March, and grow more distant
from the sun and each other
like stray, worn soldiers retreating
from an enemy that no longer exists.

It is a mild spring in Purgatory.
In green Limbo the children whose foreheads are dry,
whose hands do not grow, are transformed, themselves,
to seasons, or birds circling an obelisk
of shivering mercury. None are allowed
prey. None are allowed heaven's crooked beak.
They are radiant swallows, or hummingbirds
with thorns for tongues
to feed on the shifting mercury
from the mythology of God's hand
which I cannot break, even now,
under this tearful scrutiny.
I've tried.

I am allowing to pass through me
a statement of death.
You, the catalyst of such distorted memory.

In that Limbo the children move
in some strange gravity within and
outside grace. Their Lord is angry.
They have died with their innocence untested.

None knows what they have been,
or will be. Each day it changes
without changing. Do you understand
what I am saying? It is the life you chose
on this earth. The life of junkies and lies.

But that wasn't you. I knew you.
You had perfect lips, eyes like
a true child. Your breasts unformed.

This place where I have put you now,
It is a cursed season, an awkward
line, a flawed circle. A snake on fire
devouring what, tomorrow, it will itself become.

Prologue

Starting with little in mind
the best you might do is begin it
over and over again. Transforming

the real earth to a texture and strength
beyond control. I am thinking of a wave.

We sit, huddled in winter coats, transfixed
to the logic of stars collapsing. The fresh
gravity pulling at stones we grip.

Locked tightly to the seams of night,
the moon rears like a fenced stallion,
and, its rage subdued, turns back.

Then the hour is loose as the music,
a vapor passing through. It defies
each change. As the wind outdistances
each word spoken, and replies with
a promise already broken.

M. Verdoux, The Wife Killer

My verdict has been passed.
Now the order of my judgment draws near.

With no more questions to answer,
The time heats up. Even the past
Moves swiftly. Only small detail
Draws me into the timelessness of closed walls,

Scratching the faces of my murdered wives
Into the gravel. From the fragments
Of passing clouds I formed whole bodies
Of penitent jurors, picnicking beside a lake.
At times a single cloud appeared, shaped in each detail
To a finished image . . . a dog, a terrier reclining
With tight wire hair. Then there was the tower,

Which cast the same shadow from all angles
I remember in my youth a tower was the archetype
For wisdom and endurance. The bird which circled it
For a thousand years. And yes, I study the sounds
Of the train which passes each afternoon. Late,
When the sun is dull like her eye through that strangled veil.

Now is the morning of that day.
I hear the workers in the yard and move
To my window. The guillotine rises within
A block of stray darkness, like the blade
Of a lovely skater. I hear the signal,
The switch is thrown. My priest enters
As the bars slide open in unison, like shadows
Of my former selves, many and thin and wasted,
Marching with precision toward a passionate goal.

A Night Outing

for James Schuyler

A distance beyond
Sky's reach, membrane
Of leaf a miracle
Against my elbow

Through the tunneling light
Merging deep beneath bare ponds
With the scattering tension
Of its own blueness

Reverberation

Lifting myself
Into the silence
Of rotting bark
My calves tighten
Against soft floors
Of dead pine, two elk
Trapped in the oubliette
Of your eyes' iridescence

Listen

Earth's blue grinding
Out of thick pine
And insect ballets
Rising

The way still grey water
Throws the moon,
The cautious moon,
Right back at itself.

Wing and Claw

When I dream of you this way
You are so badly with another
I can feel his breathing
Inside these sheets.
I understand the pressure of his smell
Better than my own.

This is the moment when I am totally receptive,
Calm and unthinking under a shivering duress.

I was born for these moments,
Controlling all excess,
As if I were a skillful bird
Of prey . . . taking all I want,
yet returning for more,
Having emptied my crooked beak
And claws. It feels good
To expand so fully, talon and wing, in the path
Of the full and faithless moon.

The Ad Man's Daughter

Inside these bottles
Rows of tenements are burning.

I wait here at 5 A.M.
for the homeless
to come to our door. . . .

I hear the metallic
hum of red lights turning
green on Sixth Avenue.

Not as loud as taxis, seven flights
below, fierce with speed for dawn.
At this hour you can hear anything

It's 2 A.M. there, in N.Y.C.
where you are sleeping or awake
inside the sound of waves. The strangled wind
holds light across the bedroom window, then cuts
loose its sound, a whip that shows both ends.

Saint Theresa

Her tiny heart
pierced on a thorn
heats the jealous rose above it.

The thin stem of dried blood
spill from her palm
one by one together
like a locket from an envelope, a gift,
which soothes her Lord's unkept promises
without malice or regret. Only

a great vision remains, it uproots
The numb vines
From your clasped fist and whispered psalm.

It falls like the silence, its leaves
turned light in the purpose of your genuflection.

In Four Seasons

The seasons are a series of transparencies.
Slowly, slowly in your eyes they are aligned,
In your hand overlap. You have given up

So much grace to a fear of changing storms,
Each one's mystery requiring such different provisions,

A set of improvisations. Like the phrasing of slow,
Half-forgotten songs. To that fear you have given up your
    youth.

Winter, you saw no purity in the stillborn snow.
The landscape meant nothing to you,
Only its quick decay in your flushed fevered palm.

Summer, the sun was a relic, a coin uncovered
From some volcano's ruin. Its heat
Opened the pores of a grave which arrived by mail
As a gift in spring. And fall,

You wore that casually, a sweater fastened loosely
Around your waist. Always in case the cold arrived.
You prepared yourself for the most superfluous orders
                    of the earth and sky.

It was only those days of transformation . . . the few
Yet tempestuous In-betweens . . .
Which were gripped tightly in your hand
Like a divorced ring

Which you finally managed to remove,
Uncertain of what came next,
Though it was only the remnant
Of a failure you would never give up.

Dead Salamander's Song

The sistine eye,
The twisted thigh. If
Dead skin says nothing,
Then it cannot lie. But

Its coral breath
Could light night when alive.
And its will to outsmart
the sun was a dance
Which no language survives.

Painting by Flashlight

In a temporary room
Walls a strained yellow
Like a Japanese wrist.
Lexington below lights out,
I light a flashlight against
Utrillo. A weightless snow in
The upward strokes, that is,
The bleak branches
Thin as torn fingernails.

There is a sense
Of danger, to study a painting
With a focused beam, surrounded
By the transient darkness of hotel rooms.
As if you were a thief examining
The numbers of a safe. You step closer,

The grey building's facade
Scraped with knives from
Madmen, perhaps, fleeing music. Mauve
Bonnets on the shoeless peasant girls,

Intense as bag ladies outside at this hour
Uptown, weighing the possibilities
Of streets intersecting. But these girls

Walk in numbers, hand in hand, toward
A farther, deeper perspective. Out

And through these walls.
As the batteries burn.

Heroes
for Phil Ochs

Fallen one, your private ghosts are
stepping on you from the heights
where you left them off. Their necks are
tiered like a noose. But we don't need
that. Each eye sees a different tattoo. . . .
You changed my life. I sat in the rain
with *The New York Times* to get your act down.

Now you move
through these crowds
knowing the indulgences
Of each maneuver

like a needle
through the satin that lines
the restoration of an old, old crown.

Nightclubbing

For this generation,
infected with too many antidotes,
there must be a balcony, a height
where one may be lifted up
beyond the timorous grip of glamour,
of glory without rage,

to initiate and incite the shaded dancers
who are eager and anorexic, wearing
monkey teeth on their wrists,
lips or fingers painted black,
passing out affinity with the howling dog
And their trousseau of darts,
As the letters of their tattoos dissolve,
Leaving mermaids and flowers, the banded hearts
Stranded without vows or names. . . .

I challenge you to restore
a reckless elegance in place of
The vapors you breathe of hubris and boring
saturations of such civilized distraction . . .
to commit to sleep in a painless chamber
The tedious pets of your cradled syringes.

I can license you
the malnourished but willing
innocence of a cloudless destiny
And petition you to summon the mysteries,
With joy not envy, dissevering the crooked
Braces you insist on wearing, without blinding
You with too much at once, the forgotten elements . . .
I'm talking about a very slow first move, and carefully,

as you reach, as I reach too,
Through a wheel of thorns
To pump new air into the stray rose.

Post-Modernism

I gather up the giant holes.
Why should I bother with the rock
and sand which fills them?

Why should I bother with distracting weights
Without elegance, or allow myself to be taken
hostage, leaving only through back doors,
a gun raised to the pulse of my lucid shadow?

The Caves

I am part of these walls.
The cool moss is a calendar
to my ancient dreaming. These walls
were painted by the cycles of the moon
passing through the bodies of women.

The true signs are faded. All that remains
are the parodies of heaven, all that remain
are the bison and stag, a briefing for the hunt,

an inventory. Yet night and the fire
can reinvent the screams. Tracing my hands
across the veins of fury. Gripping the bone
of a generation which was shaped by its child
into the head of an arrow.

Judging the Pageant

The sun splits into two
like a futurist eye.
You may have your choice of either.
I'll take what's left.
You know my indifference
That's why I was chosen. Now watch:

One sets west
this evening on a line
where the ocean departs, serious
And loose, a flamingo bending to feed
from the cupped palm of the horizon.

The sun set east
like a jealous twin
This evening: another horizon, rigid
And dense, a coin stuck halfway
In the slot of a glass tank. Remember . . .

the coin's on fire,

And your choice is final.
No matter to me.
All I want is your reason. Between the two,
all I care for is the difference.

El Hombre del Ombre

Take the letter "H" from a Spanish
man on the streets of Madrid
in his native tongue

And that man will become
a shadow among the French.

A Window in Cherry Valley

Across the pond
reeds bow against
the soft charge of night

change

further down
they are fingers
inviting me to the pleasures
of death by water

Its split-second
passion, its surrendered
sound of exploding lungs

like poor bells ringing
underwater and
it's late at night

On Tour

Each night another room
without changing, the white
walls grow less bright, like
color returning to the joints
of a hand that feared flying
but no longer cared.

It comes with a Bible and
a print of Paris under grey
winter, women walking in couples
toward a monument that endures,
room to room. Night to night,
the faces of the women grow closer.
I am trying to read their lips.
Give me a week and I'll succeed.
And I'll regret having done it.
For now I make out a single word
and a name . . . "Caesar Augustus"
and "abattoir."

Aside from this
There is little else. . . .
I get in late
And sleep until someone calls.

Then I go, leaving everything
As it was . . . a bed, a bright-
colored chair. Perhaps a desk.

It's like a poem.
The smaller the room
The neater it must be
Once you're done with it.

Dueling the Monkey
for Lou and Sylvia Reed

The fair lady works at shuttles
Brush knee and twist step
Play the lute
Part the wild horse's mane

Golden cock stands on one leg
Watch with fist under elbow
Lift hand
Insert needle to sea bottom

Step back and repulse monkey
Flash the arms (unfurl the fan)
Separate your instep
Left and right

Stork spreads wings
Turn and strike with heel
Paint the bottled fly
Strike tiger left and right

Turn around and cast away your fist and palm
Blow ears
Dodge and kick
Sweep lotus with a single hand

Step forward to form seven stars
Press face with vanquished palm
Brush knee and underbelly
Stand back, deflect, parry, and punch

Cross form and ride stork
Step back, seeming close-up
Lift hand
Embrace tiger and return to mountain.

A Child Growing Up with the Sun

The sun sits back, watches the street
like an informant for the junta.
By now, I understand each motive
in the sky, and its shadows on earth.

I am helpless nonetheless. It's tough
when an immense power cannot be terrorized.
When it is invulnerable to a slip of madness.

I acknowledge its brilliance, as I was left, by choice
to shadows. And in that shelter, I dreamt.
I spent my youth's desires like a peculiar currency.
It was a running joke between myselves,
the one I believed in, and each of the others.

It confessed its innocence to me
through Mayakovsky's poem. Once,
It poisoned my skin in the Rockaways
to get my attention. I took it for granted.

That was a magnificent mistake.

I never learned to trust it. I wore dark
glasses, disguised my skin in hats with wide brims.
It knew too much, its vantage points always
too well chosen. Where did it go at night?
thought the child, and who did it meet and what, exactly,
did it have to report? So they grew, these suspicions,
as one. And I chose, instead, the dark dance of the moon.
In the face of two, I have always sought the lesser majesty.

For John Donne

Stars, in their unchecked lust,
ejaculate still onto the barren moons
their pulsating milk. The solar winds

like Aurora seeds, enter
At the poles of this planet, above and below.

Don't you see
the obscenity of glaciers, waiting like
aged dictators, blinding white,
impatient for their cycle to devour?

Born of this,
we watch night grow,
voyeurs of cloudless nights,
impatient and pathetic
to imitate its pleasures, to uncover

the code of its birth.

Eugene, Oregon

for Judith and Aeron

The promise
Within a cloud . . . Rain?
Small gods in jealous turmoil?
Scale? Hypnosis?

Rain,
I hope. Then
I'll find the plum

leaves across the sidewalks,
Small, crescent and wet

To peel cautiously
Up as they press
The pavement like forged labels
from bottles of pills
To sleep outside the law.

Like scaled decals
For a child's serious
model airplane or ship,

Like flags to signal
Danger from the bridge
In high water, our engines gone.

Our Desires

There is a wind that seeks the crevice
under my heart
the way insects file at night
beneath a doorway

Its edges are rough, it slits
the cords. It trips my steady breathing.
When it comes there is no one
I can trust.

It seems, at times, I have designed
too well this vision of you.
I cannot survive your eyes
when they are scarred with a need
for some lesser form of love.

I admit to this conceit.
And though you will not accept it
You love it nonetheless

It is just like you. Our desires
will always be kept sharp
by a kind of perversity. A need
to be each forever alone. . . .

Its color is violet, like lips
that have been smashed by night
or robbed of blood by lack of breath.
The wind I was speaking of does this.

I can feel it now.

My Debt

for V.S.

I come to your bedroom door.
I come slowly, and alone. A scented wind
Pins me. It seems ominous, but I'm not sure.
It is as if a document were posted there
In some obscure language, revealing all and nothing.

I need to cry out,
Loud and anonymous,
Off the crumbling walls of Western night . . .
If I could disguise my scream
Like a distant jackal beneath uncertain moons
I could ride awhile on time alone.
It is my right.

But the tribe of this language,
Of these words, is finished.
It is the long cry, now, of the dead.

A ghost be my translator . . . but the ghosts
Owe me nothing. I have no justice here.
I am asking for too much.

But I did come to your door.
I came slowly and alone.

On Susan's Birthday

Brown woman with watermarked eyes
lay beside me on polished teakwood

That's all I remember of the city . . .

Spanish boots choke her thighs
like slick vines, a Roman nose
that breathes only the scent of burning orange
her eyes drip like bleeding almonds

A passion for excessive detail
leans like a crucifix between her breasts

She skims her fingers up my cheek softly
like stones across sleeping water

This is where I reach her
not in the flame but in the pool
of a wet dream always and just after dawn

when the sunlight hesitating
at the window

is a shadow outdone by the purer light
pumped upward between your thighs

Poem

It's sad this vision required
    such height.
I'd have preferred to be down
With the others
    in the stadium.

They know the terror of birds.

I am left, instead, with the deep
    drone . . .
The urgency to deliver light, at least
    a fragment, as if it

Were news from the far galaxies.

Dresden to Chesapeake Bay

The train sits airtight
beneath the Chesapeake Bay.
The nets are rising above.
Again he dreams the Dresden dream

Of her, surfacing
from a basement filled with the skin
of oranges, wet and loose beneath the shattered
pipes. She climbs the wooden stairs, in a borrowed gown

and he follows
down streets, each lonelier
Than the one before.

There are no flames, only wheels,
detached and rolling,
a vicious red route through smoke
faster than the panting
of cheetahs breathing to the scent,
tracking deer flesh. She surfaces

far and near,
sooner or later, destination unclear.
He hears through the engine
Of his plane the curve
of another terrible horizon, guilty
For not yet being born.

In the Deep Green Vase

The petals of a soft yellow rose
speak urgently, as if they were labels
sewn by fierce young girls, held captive,
with the suture of their wounds.

Here in Ward number six,
in the corridor in the deep
green vase, grows another rose,
younger and more subtle in its cautious bloom.

Its irony is the way it has strained
To achieve the sublime.

Perhaps it is like me.
Perhaps it is afraid of light
and dreaming by day.

Its color is that of the lips
of a young mute girl
they allowed to return
home for winter, her hands
still at work, stitching day and night.
This, her final season, her finished desire
distributing the contraband of roses
smuggled from the deep green vase.

Poem

I snatch a grape from her breast
as a drunk steals apples
he will never eat.

In a dark room
the eyes of tearful birds glow

and it is cold there
your breasts shrink like nerves exposed
to the whisper of spiders hanging
from fixtures of attic light.

Seferis knows this place
and his ancestors
whose faces are dented
by the wind of mythology.

How often can a man be rebuilt?
For my part, I feel petals of zinc
clogging my pores.

You would appear better off,
hair mixing with sunlight on sand,
but you wear a longing for death
tightly across your forehead
like the mask of a surgeon.

In pools that sing on the mountain of sleeping maidens
I party with the ghosts of my heritage.
Some sing in German, some sing the song of Druids,
they do not recognize me, and they do not care . . .
they will feed my flames to the cold winds of night.

The New Death
for Ebbe Borregaard

I.

I see it passing
in silicon deserts.

It cannot slow down
though, at times
I will gather enough speed

to fix my motion
onto its tracks

and gather its eyes
like dice
into my fist

to weigh the vision there
against my own.

II.

Its power to deceive
can burn or freeze,

Can easily slip away.

It studies its maneuvers
in my own eyes.

It charges itself
in my strength.

As I tighten the grip

It throws me, broken,
into the dancing chaparral

to choke me with chaste laughter,
and presses my lips deep

into the dreams of ants feasting.

III.

Found it once more in the ocean's rush

Laying myself convicted
in moon-spiked surf,

Coasting foam and salt spray
ripping the ear deep,

I hear the death clock ticking there like dried bones.

It handles the darkness well
and smashes it across my ribs like a gull's scream.

It clings to torn fingers
like fetus flesh.

I want to fling it deep
into tides of lunar madness

But it rides these waves clean
like a flawless surfer

And dances a new death
across the stones . . .

where I summon the rays which cry from the crevice.

The Runners

I.

You hear the call,
the struggle of winter.

I watch the shapes of shade
which run from children
like frightened birds, children

who crossed the line of peculiar night
without warning, or proper humility.

II.

Their voice, as one, was heavy
like words flung across a swamp.

Then the voices broke, overlapped
and ran. As the swamp began to run,
becoming a stream, clear and dangerous.

III.

Thick as milk from a peasant's breast,
gravity presses them to this floor,
a carpet of moss and stone. Then they think
with a painful clarity, the clarity
of a heretic's flames.

IV.

Here, every lost act,
no matter how distant in the mind,
ends in murder.

3 Short Poems

Poem

Some trust the wolf
they have raised since birth
not to turn on them.

Some trust their lives
In the hands whose fingers
Are five silent knives.

Some will be reminded
of nothing, or perish
By that memory.

Compassion

Stepfather, I wanted
to spit in your mouth
as you lay in that casket,
to put beneath your tongue

some drops of the moisture
which you scream for this moment
in the piles of hell.

Cinco de Mayo

I live in these hills, made heavy
     with tanks, their tracks
         Leave pools where small, round fish
         Like coins with wings swim as if
         In the footprints of thunder. Here

Every day is Cinco de Mayo.
Everywhere is the Equator. Every hour,

motionless above women and men, the sun
watches or waits like a god or a threat.

Things That Fly

I.

My blond niece speaks in riddles
to her uncaged bird

Like Francis of Assisi and his flock
of wolves, a shining mist at dawn descends
like a wall to words between them.

II.

Misery may be folded
in half, like a sheet
of blank paper. Or filled
With words. No matter.
It is only a first step.

You must continue the folds, parallel
To each side, until their intricacy
builds on itself, forms a delicate
grace. Separate. Facing itself.

In Japan, there are beautiful words
For each step. This way misery dies

in equal parts, until it forms
a paper missile at twelve noon
to fling out any window, without
aiming. But only from a great height.

For Robert Smithson

A hummingbird, slow through the camera,
drinks fame from the blistered hand of a tower

In midtown Manhattan. In Mojave, desert flowers
grind their teeth for midday.
Between the breathless flags
Of the canyon, only the tumors
Survive. Only the cracked skull
of cattle, their shadows perfect

triangles. You told me one night,
only the most casual humor
fit when you were drunk at Max's. Out there,
only the spiral stones, laid out in serious
colors, like the crossing of ghostly tribes . . .

arranged like the letters of some lost language
on the jetty. How perfect your last
Vision of them from above, a part

of the air there, too light for your wings.

Borges Death Mask

We become the children
Of a dream that recurs over time.

The lips of the mask
Were white as the finished flame
Of fire in some concentric ruins,

Its eyes pale red
like the tongue of
A caged white bear.

Its features were simple,
the drawings of children left alone
To live along the blacktop of a schoolyard,

shaded like those
whose final will
initiates our dreams.

I call them father.
I wear a mask.

The Desert Casino

I pour water slowly
into the fragile vase of your lungs.
The seeds burst upward
from your heart. You are an extravagance.
Flowers push

finally, by morning
through the black soil
of your breath,
out of your lips.

Never stop. Never. Now

I put on you, like a gaudy cape,
long, long sleep.
You dream in German. I answer
with the sound of scissors sharpening.

It is becoming too much for me, this life
around the desert casino. I throw buckets
of sterile buds
of mariposa
blood-lilies
into the pavilions of cacti and mirrors
at dawn. I sit,

a salamander on the hood
of a pale blue Chevrolet
in outraged heat, tired of the obsessions

for passion, and the small, sleek ornament of risk.

The jagged pieces
Of last night's games lie
Across the checkered sand with
The shattered teeth of coyote.

Music Television

The cable rises
up the midtown
Building's facade like vines
ascending virgin trees above
the hills of Fatima, the grotto
at Lourdes. The wires are attached

with great care, the last
module inserted delicately
like the final stone in an altar,
that one anointed, filled with relics
of saints, delivered in vast
European processions. Finally

the knob is turned. Music
arrives before the image
appears. Only a moment,
confusing to the faithful,

And the screen glows
like X-rays, revealing
the bones of some martyr's
shriveled fingers, then a blond
woman in stripes, then a living
hand, painted blue . . . everyone's
watching. It seems to be working.

What could I have been thinking of,
saying
what I said?

Sleeplessness

Without sleep, without dreaming,
How can I break you down?

Is it sympathy or envy
That causes me to wait up, bedside
With a pale, anorexic moon?

I wake you; cover your eyes
With postage stamps painted with owls
For the commemoration of insomnia.

I have come to accept, in these hours,
The rules of an efficient terror. In these hours,
Which repeat nightly the same precision,
Which are louder than the rest. The sound of
These clocks like birds across a tin lawn.
The cat smashing his paw against the TV
Screen, as a missile arcs across the background
Of a flag. The station "signing off."
Just like me.

In the Gears

Of the jungle
In the desecration of the iris
In bloom for images juxtaposed
In the quasar mist, the mitre
Of white dwarves, the bishop's claw
In the conclave of authority
Among straining stars

I abjure all velocity as I shatter
Each commitment, the words in vanished gold
inlaid in walls like Mexican teeth.

In the birdcage beneath my ribs
In the panic of the hummingbird
As it swallows my heart
Through the sly thorn of its beak

In the compromise of the clock
In the hour hand's folding
Across seconds like trapped ells

In the harmless crystal made
Mad on your lips, sewn by decay
And night, in the emblem
Of pedants with exploding luggage
and gauges for elegance,
In the subscription of hearts
In the strangled teeth of work
In the judgment of each word
In the end, pretend you hear me.

New Work 1989–1993

Curtis's Charm

I ran into my old friend Curtis yesterday, way uptown—the edges of Harlem. We'd been on a drug detox program together many years ago, long before they became fashionable and assumed the look of Ivy League campuses. We got fairly tight then . . . everyone did in those bleak surroundings.

Curtis had the same look as back then: long straggly goatee like some Chinese astrologer. A shaved head, giving him a remarkable resemblance to the boxer Marvin Hagler (though only about half his size).

I saw Curtis coming from a block away, heading downtown on Fifth with that cranked, purposeful walk of a purposeless man. He was cutting through the humidity with rocking elbows, auto-cruising on major fear and bad crack. Dangerously bad crack, speed-laced, dearly in want of sedative grace.

He was wearing the same hat he had on at our last chance meeting six years ago—a short-billed black beanie, leather. He told me that the blue zippered jacket and dark blue baggy trousers I was wearing made me look like I was on a work detail from Riker's Island. After asking about mutual colleagues from the old days and other musings, Curtis came up square on me with his eyes. Serious contact. Urgent. The whites of those eyes were as yellow as an old sheep's. I envied the man's teeth, however. He asked me if I was in any rush; said that he was involved in a situation which I might be able to help with. "You be just who I need talking to right now," he spoke, just above a whisper.

We crossed Fifth Avenue and walked down the stairs leading into one of the secret jewels of Central Park, the Conservatory Gardens. All the flowers were blooming full, all the benches were empty. Except for a suspicious park worker grooming the curve of a hedge with huge, brutal shears, it seemed we two were alone. We took a bench near the back gate, surrounded by high rows of pink mums, and surveyed the hordes of flora. I mentioned that these gardens were the place where Ben E. King came to get into the lyric of "Rose in Spanish Harlem" the morning before recording it.

"What ever happened to Joe Tex?" Curtis asked, by way of a non sequitur reply.

"No idea," I answered.

243

"See if you can find out," he said, almost as a command.

"You know," he went on, "I heard that James Brown once offered to pay for one of those sex change operations for Joe Tex, so that he could marry him as a bitch. He said he loved Joe's voice so damn much that he wanted to get down with him, but not like a faggot, dig? He wanted to marry him so as all be right in God's eyes and shit. You ever hear that?"

I hadn't, but I said that I had.

Then Curtis shot me another look that said it was time to cut through the chitchat. The guy with the giant shears was getting closer; the sound of his furious snipping getting loud and frightful in the silent, sweet-scented air.

Curtis is badly troubled. He's in a place where, for once, his street smarts and weaponry don't fit in nor do any good. As his tale tells, he's convinced that his new Caribbean mother-in-law, an adept of the dark tricks, is tagging him with sundry spells of heavy voodoo Ju-Ju. He claims he can feel the curse infiltrating his brain like flaming arrows through his ears.

His wife told him that because he's been seeing other women and spending the money designated for groceries and Pampers on crack, that now her mother is going to settle the score with various incantations and magic brews. He tells me that, right as we are speaking, there is a small brass crucible in the old hag's apartment with his name on it, and with his photo and some snippings from his privates resting within.

"And any hour now," he states, pacing back and forth (nearly trampling a row of peach hibiscus), "this old bitch's gonna take something from one of them voodoo supply jars she got all over the house and toss it onto my picture in that there bowl. My wife says that if it be some kinda herbs or shit tossed in, then I be all right . . . that all it gonna do is straighten me out . . . you know, smarten up my ass and keep me in line.

"But if her moms wants to really get down to business, then she gonna take a scorpion, or some other creep poison bug, from them jars, and then I gonna be one sorry-ass black man, hurting like a mo'fo' and there ain't nothin'—not a damn thing—that any straight-up doctor can do."

I was shifting all over the bench during Curtis's rant. His fear was genuine, his eyes widely palpitant with it. And I knew, now that he had opened the ventilation shaft, that I was in this problem for the long haul. It wasn't the type of day I wanted to spend disarming delusion either. It was only 10:30 A.M., but the grace period of cooler morning air had disappeared. The temperature was heading toward the mid-nineties again and the humidity was conjuring steam from the garden growth. The well-tended, even lines of flora suddenly seemed more like a virgin rain forest. The sweat from Curtis's black pores flowed free from his face as the porous neurons of madness, demons, and drugs fired through his mind. It seemed yellow-tinted, this sweat, as if from years of orange methadone biscuits and bad cocaine cut.

"Listen," he went on. "I know what you're thinking, but I know that this woman's shit be working on me already. Like, I been doing some weird stuff lately, or better said, some weird shit's been being done to me.

"The other week, I passed out smoking a plain old joint, and *two days later* I woke up in some rotten homeless men's shelter in *Queens*! In Queens, man, dig that! I ain't never been to Queens before that. Caused all sorts of problems. I missed my face-to-face down at Welfare and they held up my digit for eight damn days. Got in trouble at the methadone clinic, as well. They went and lowered my dose, so now each bottle I sell on the street be worth five dollars less than before.

"And when I get home and tell my wife what happened and why I was gone, she tells me, all nonchalant, that I just got hold of some bad grass . . . like it had been angel-dusted or some such nonsense. But I know, goddamn it, that it was her momma at work with her evil shit.

"But all that's chump stuff compared to what came next. Worse by far is what I've been *seeing* lately. Now, first of all, let me explain one thing. You see, I know that my wife's been stealing money out of my trouser pockets at night after I put on my house-shorts. So I been hiding the bread the last couple of weeks. But it don't do no good, because with her powers, my wife's old lady can see where it be hid, by rattling some beads and looking into this bowl of green water she got on her living room table. And she tells my wife. But even if I keep a twenty-four-hour eye on the bitch, I can't stop her from taking the money because—and don't you laugh man 'cause what I'm telling you be true; I saw it and I'm counting on you to help 'cause I figure you know about weird shit, and I can't talk about this to anyone else. You see, I can't stop her from stealing my stash because now she got the powers from her momma . . . or maybe it's the old lady herself coming over at night to my apartment . . . but one of them, somehow, *knows how to change into an animal.*

"And not just one kind of animal, but any kind of animal they want to be, no fucking lie. Because three days ago, only about eight blocks from right here, I saw this squirrel jump off a tree limb from Central Park onto the sidewalk on Fifth Avenue, and I'm sure, I'm positive, that little furry mo'fo' was following me down 108th Street, all the way to Third Avenue, while I was scoring some dimes of rock. Now when was the last time you saw a squirrel on Third Avenue, man? And the way that little sucker was looking at me, you know, sitting up on its hind legs like they do? You wouldn't believe it, man."

I didn't, but said nothing as Curtis paused in his astonishing rap. The guy with the shears was working much too hard for a city employee in high humidity. The *swish* . . . *clang* sound was so loud that Curtis almost had to yell the last part of his story.

We both stared at the guy; he sped up his act, staring straight back at us with a sick, defiant smile. Curtis freaked. He ran over to a trash can and loaded up with three or four empty soda cans, which he proceeded to wing at the guy in rapid succession. "He's one of them, man," Curtis yelled over to me as he continued to fling crushed aluminum. "He works for the old lady."

I grabbed Curtis while the besieged gardener ducked out of sight behind a hedge, and led him out the back gate. We ran up a hill and over some rocks, finally collapsing in totally-out-of-shape exhaustion on a grass patch beside a secluded path.

"Sorry man," Curtis spoke in half breaths. "It was just that I didn't like the way he smiled. It was evil."

"I think he was a cop, Curtis," my voice flared up. "He probably just thought we were getting high. You got to control yourself."

"You're most likely right." Curtis looked up, all settled in a crouch position now, wanting back my full attention. "Well, fuck that dude anyway . . . where was I?"

"You were being spied on, while purchasing drugs, by a squirrel," I answered.

"Right, but that was only the start." He took a look around, then continued.

"Last night was much stranger. Listen here: last night I was sitting at home in my good chair, feet up, watching a cowboy movie, and what do I see? On a bible, now, I'm swearing to this: right in my living room come this little black mouse—a shade of black the same as my wife, come to think of it—moving across the floor right beside the wall, *with a ten dollar bill in its mouth!*

"It was stopping after every ten feet or so, looking around all sneaky, just like a thief . . . *with a ten dollar bill in its mouth, man.* And it was coming straight from the direction of the loose plastic brick at the bottom of the phony fireplace where I been hiding my money. I looked over at the brick and could tell it had been moved just a tiny crack.

"So I got up to chase the little mo'fo' and it splits around the corner, then right under the bedroom door. I fling the door open and it's gone, nowhere in sight, and my wife is just laid out on the bed, all naked and chilled, with a big shit-eating grin on her face. I know she had that ten dollar bill stashed somewhere, and I know the only reason she be naked was because she'd just changed back from being the mouse and didn't have no time yet to put something on.

"So you tell me, man, can her momma, or anyone, have the power to change someone into a mouse, or a squirrel? You tell me, 'cause if the old bitch can do that, then I know any curse she wants to put on me is gonna work, and my butt be burning."

Curtis looked up at me in wounded-animal terror. The expression on his face was like that of an onlooker at a lynching in some gray turn-of-the-century photograph. I knew now that my old friend Curtis's fears were, in his mind, very real and, if anything, had become a perfect ally for the mother's sympathetic magic, real or imagined.

He asked again if I thought such powers of transmutation possible

. . . if I'd read about that and these voodoo spells and curses. I told him how shape-shifting was big in the Middle Ages, but had pretty much petered out as of late, after making a short and abortive comeback in the late 1800s in France. I assured him that, even if her credentials were genuine, it was not at all likely his mother-in-law could turn his wife into either mouse or squirrel. Then I explained what I knew regarding homeopathic magic, breaking it down into its subsections of contagious and sympathetic magic. This was all pretty much out of *The Golden Bough*, and I realized halfway through it was a bit too academic for Curtis's benefit, under the circumstances. He just wanted to know if the old lady's curses were going to work, and, that being the case, what he could do in self-defense.

"See, that's just the point," I spoke up. "The worst thing you can do about any of this black magic shit is let yourself believe it works, and that you got no defense against it. Once you let that notion inside your head, then you're just gonna get paranoid and help it along. It's like they plant this seed of self-destruction inside you, and your sense of helplessness just waters the thing. The thing to do is think righteously and purify yourself, then any curse aimed at you will be thrown back off you and returned to the sender, working against her seven times stronger than when it was sent."

"How am I supposed to purify myself at this point, man? I mean, we're like two germs talking to each other."

He had a point, though I took umbrage at Curtis classifying me on an equal basis of "germ" as himself. I convinced him that I had made great strides since we first knew each other, as drug-infested microbes, toward "purifying" myself . . . at least to the degree where I could deal efficaciously against the forces of evil which he had incurred.

Whether or not this claim had any validity was irrelevant, and my reasons for putting the idea forth were not as petty as they might, at first, seem. The fact is that I had come up with a *plan*, and one of its essential aspects was gaining my man Curtis's unswerving belief that I had the power to carry it through.

The situation was clear. I had no chance of assuaging Curtis's terror by any psychobabble pep talks. He wasn't buying that shit, and who could blame him? He'd been tailed by a squirrel, and stood by helplessly as an Afro-mouse, who was his wife, raided his stash and made off with a ten dollar bill.

I was gonna fight Curtis's battle on a fire versus fire, or magic versus magic, basis. I'd match her spell for spell. In my sudden enthusiasm, I blocked out the possibility that his adversary might be horribly genuine, that my face, name, and address might be at this moment showing up clearly on the surface of her bowl of green water. *And what about* the dude with the loud gardening shears? Like I said before: no city worker works that fastidiously in that much heat.

No matter. I had, if not exactly purity, then stupidity and good intentions on my side. And a plan.

We started walking; I wanted to think on the move. Just as we were about to reach the large open meadow at 100th Street, however, we stumbled onto another frightful detour. At the base of a jagged boulder, its facade illuminated in red by some indecipherable glyphs, were three headless chickens. They didn't seem too old, though the open-neck cavities were being furiously traversed by about a dozen species of insects, busy and buzzing. Black candle stubs were scattered about, along with several half-smoked cigars. It was obviously the remnants of some ritual, a small oblation to some three-thousand-year-old Congolese river goddess. I suppose the old axiom holds true for elemental gods as well as old artists: If you continue to do anything long enough, people will begin to take you seriously.

All this dark synchronicity was becoming a bit tiresome. Was there any fucking glen or glade in this park without the vestiges of that old black magic?

I looked up at Curtis; he was gone. I saw him waving from a bench about two hundred yards away, on the edge of the meadow. Apparently the headless-chickens scene had inspired a dash out of Curtis that any world class sprinter could have envied. I sat down beside him on the bench, surveying the big, open field. It felt good seeing little wholesome kids playing whiffle ball with their dads, probably all divorced and out on their visitation day. Nothing spooky here.

I took out my mini-notepad and ripped out a blank page. I held it up in front of Curtis's face, that same strange sweat just moaning from his pores.

249

"Now we can take care of business, man. Putting aside all the bullshit of 'why' and 'how,' what you need is some magic of your own . . . some sort of protective charm or talisman, to block out this insinuating evil and neutralize it for good."

"That be exactly what I need!" Curtis perked up. "That's what I wanted all along, but can you do it?"

"Can I do it?" I sneered, my tone rebuking him for his doubts. "Of course I can do it. Man, you got to trust me." My main mission, at this point, was instilling total belief in the spiritual sleight of hand which I was winging.

"I've got a spell to match anything the dark force can toss your way, proven and powerful. I picked it up from this great holy man on the Island of Cyprus. They call him 'The Magus of Strovolos.' "

Curtis was visibly impressed by this arcane sounding appellation. I had his attention and complete confidence. Actually, the Magus does indeed exist, as does the prescription for protection I was about to lay on Curtis. As for how legitimate its powers were, I could not really say since I'd only read about it in a book about the holy man. Certainly, it had the simplicity, precision, and elegance of a prayer —quite genuine, to both the heart and the mind. Naturally, whether I possessed any semblance of the purity of spirit essential to performing the task was another matter altogether.

I bent down on one knee and laid my notepaper across a day-old *New York Post*. I realized the moment I first laid my felt-tip down that I must have had more faith in the Magus than I realized, because I suddenly felt overwhelmed by a sense of blasphemy. Referring again to what I'd read in *The Magus of Strovolos*, I shut my eyes and pictured a ball of white light unwinding from my hand and surrounding my entire body. Still I heard the tiny voice in my head repeating the phrase: *"You kidding me?"*

I looked up at Curtis. I was now really pissed off that he had dragged me into this shit.

But I'd waved the blank paper as a promise in his face, and I had to deliver. I began forming the lines on the paper. First symbol was the Star of David, centered in the bottom half of the page. Then around it I drew four small crosses: north, south, east, west. Beneath each cross I printed the names of the four hierarchical archangels:

Michael, Raphael, Ariel, and Gabriel. I confess that there was a specific clockwise order to these names—corresponding, I believe, to the four elements as well as the compass points—but I couldn't remember who went where, so I began with Michael on top and then continued randomly from there. That was the bottom half of the charm. It was sort of a preparatory incantation . . . a sort of spirit-battery. I held it up to Curtis. "This is the source of power. Now, above it, we address the evil that's challenging you."

I began on the upper half, Curtis scoping in tightly over my shoulder. The first designation here was a snake. Up until now, everything was straight lines and letters, but this required some slight ability of basic draughtsmanship, a gift which I have never possessed. Nevertheless, I got on with it, and the results seemed satisfactory enough to me. As I lifted the pen a moment, however, Curtis snatched the paper up and held it between us, hand trembling.

"What you doing drawing a picture of a *dick*, man?" he exclaimed vehemently. "I thought this be good magic . . . holy and good."

"That's a snake, not a damn dick," I sighed, lifting the paper out of his hand. "Here, let me fix it up a bit."

I embellished some rings around my snake rendering, then added a rattle on its tail and a long forked tongue darting all nasty from its mouth. I held it up again for Curtis's perusal.

"Still looks more like a dick than a snake," Curtis went on, "just got a fork coming out its tip now."

"Listen, man, it's just a *symbol*, you know," I shot back, peeved. "I ain't no photorealist, okay?" Besides, maybe that's what your dick looks like, but not mine."

I was down to the last sign. I drew a bolt of lightning, which started from the very top of the page and passed right through the snake's neck. It continued on to mid-page and ended. A righteous zapping of the serpentine evil archetypes by the Celestial Hierarchies.

I had Curtis sign the spell in the bottom corner, then I folded it in a series of elaborate angles. It was supposed to wind up as a neat, tiny pyramid of paper, but it came out more like some prehensile trapezoid. No matter, it was close enough. Curtis accepted it with a reverence and relief. "Now I got the mojo," he exclaimed, placing it in his pocket.

"Don't flaunt it, Curtis," I told him. "By the way, according to the Magus, you have to take it to church and sprinkle a little holy water over it. It's important . . . any Catholic church carries the stuff."

Whatever the real potency of the Magus's diagram, its effect on Curtis was exactly what I'd hoped for. His faith in the folded charm was absolute; his hands kept caressing the pocket which held it. I was wiped out . . . wanted to get away from there and soak my brain into something fresh and forgetful.

We came out of the park at 98th Street and Fifth. Curtis split uptown, turning around every twenty feet or so with some gesture of thanks. I stood watching him a short while, then headed down 98th Street over to Madison to pick up a paper.

Finally free of Curtis's presence and concerns, I was swamped with speedily vacillating thoughts and feelings during this one-block walk: the power of evil, the power of goodness, the extent of a joke's success. What if I was feeling some legitimate sense of faith, no matter how disarrayed? There was nothing wrong with that. The small voice again: "You kidding me?"

I reached the corner, fairly much neutralizing these rival, racing thoughts, which had all pulled up lame far before reaching the finish line.

Suddenly I thought of *The Tempest*:

But this rough magic I here abjure . . .

I paid for the paper in one of those Korean combination newspaper-and-tobacco/stationery/groceries/small-notions/and-salad-bar stores on the corner of Madison. What I saw as I exited the place just froze me on the spot. It actually felt like someone had smashed something rare and made of blue blown glass inside my brain. I did my first Manhattan double-take in about fifteen years.

Lying right there on the sidewalk, busy with lunchtime staffers from Mt. Sinai Hospital, was a snake. It was dead, of course, and only about nine inches long, but there it was. And how long could it have been there? Certainly no fastidious, eagle-eyed Korean merchant with a staff of fourteen relatives would allow a dead snake to linger very long right in front of his establishment.

Question: When was the last time you saw a snake in Manhattan? I grew up here, and I've never before seen a snake on a sidewalk, not in any borough (including Staten Island). I've never seen one in a park either. In all my years walking New York City, this was the first snake I'd seen.

At this point, I'm not buying any notion of coincidence: snake in Magus's instructions, snake in drawing, snake on sidewalk one block away.

I moved over and checked closer. Once again, the blue glass rattled in my brain, as I saw how it had been killed. Its body had been severed right at the neck . . . only a few strands of fiber and sinew held the head together with the remainder of its body: body of snake on sidewalk one block away sliced straight at neck . . . body of snake in talisman pierced at neck by lightning bolt of occult elemental righteousness. *"You kidding me?"*

I started to act hyper and strange. I wanted to catch up to Curtis and let him see this scene for himself. I needed corroboration. Apparently, I began thinking, I possess powers of some elect few, great gifts from the psycho-poetic realms. There could be money in it. I eyed an empty storefront across the street. I needed Curtis as witness, to pass the word on to others.

I grabbed a Korean stacking newspapers in front of the store. "Don't let anything happen to that snake . . . do you understand me? I'll be right back?" He pulled away and ran inside. "Screw it," I yelled, running over and swiping up the filthy reptile from the sidewalk. I held it at arm's length before me with both hands, the head in one, the body in the other. It was essential the two sections didn't come apart now.

I ran over to Fifth Avenue and up to 103rd Street, fingers pointing at me from every direction. Finally, I realized there was no way I was going to find Curtis. Also, complete exhaustion from my run had sobered me considerably. I was a man holding a dead snake (with tenderish care) on a busy street lined with buses and their gawking passengers.

253

I went a few feet to the park wall and tossed the snake beneath a bush, once again abjuring the rough magic. If I did have a staff, however, I would neither break nor bury it, and as for the Magus books, I had no intention of drowning them.

Update

It's been two months now since my adventure with Curtis in Central Park. I've been trying to find him, both to fill him in on the subsequent events of that strange day and to find out what his present situation is. I've had no success, however, and don't imagine I will. According to a mutual friend I saw two nights ago, Curtis has been seen by no one, having, a month before, fled the jurisdiction of New York City authorities and a charge of burning out the guts of the entire building in which his wife was, along with her mother, presently residing. Fortunately, nobody was injured in the blaze, though the mother-in-law's irreplaceable collection of Caribbean esoterica, as well as a small menagerie of reptiles, rodents, and insects, was completely destroyed. Whether Curtis ever took the time and effort to locate the prescribed holy water and sprinkle it on the talisman, I cannot say.

I, for one, would like to know the answer.

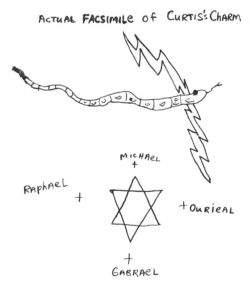

ACTUAL FACSIMILE of CURTIS's CHARM

MICHAEL
+

RAPHAEL
+

+ OURIEAL

+
GABRAEL

A Perfect Stranger

Billy didn't pay any attention to the incident behind him. The kid beside him, probably about nineteen, certainly had: he was pinching the muscles on his neck now, strained from craning his head to take it all in.

"I'm a writer," the kid turned to Billy. "Everything fascinates me."

"Oh, really," Billy answered, still staring straight ahead, up where the image of the belt buckle had disappeared. He missed it.

The young writer took the terse response and the lack of any fascination on Billy's face as a clear indication that any further conversation with the man beside him was out of the question. That was okay. He could respect that. He felt that way himself at times.

"This ride is going to suck," he thought.

Billy turned his head to the window to completely seal himself off. Just outside, the air was filled with holes the size of a large nail's head. The bigger sky in the distance seemed cleft, running vertical. Small holes near, large holes—tears, actually—off far. Ready to be ascended by some healthy kid in a stocking cap, he thought. It was unsettling. It should be horizontal from up here. His heart began to race.

Billy shifted and faced the kid, startling him with large, palpitant eyes, humming with distortion.

"How many people have you disappointed?" Billy asked, each word separate and serious.

The kid considered the question and the gestures to accompany his response. Billy was rotating his hand in the space between their stares, urging quick, fastidious thought. The kid raised his eyes and began counting on his fingers, until he got stuck on his left ring finger, extending it, touching it with his right forefinger, and then withdrawing it. He did this several times. Billy frowned, rotated his hands faster. The kid made two fists and dropped them softly into his lap.

"Seven for sure," the young writer answered, his eyes on his fingers which were manipulating the seat buckle, "Maybe eight, it depends . . . Hmmm, okay. I'll say—I'll say eight. Eight people."

He faced Billy. Billy was right there waiting.

"I've disappointed thousands." Billy spoke firmly, slowly, right at the kid, who seemed suddenly so much younger in every feature, but in his lips especially. "Literally thousands."

I Am Not Kurt Schwitters

I am not Kurt Schwitters

I am not a blue rider
Tracking the German cobblestone
Streets in snow in the old
Part of town, a port nowhere near.

I am not Sal Mineo.

I am not Bernard of Clairvaux,
Nor Abelard, for that matter.

I am not the stooped woman before dawn
Beneath the bridge and platform lights
At the *Spit* of the Devil station
Waiting too early for the train
Comes much later.

I am not the moon tonight
Thin, crescent, serrated
Like a Yemenite dagger.

I am not Leo Szilard at the red traffic light.

I am not what I am
Not
A wren on my fire escape.

I am not Taras Bulba,
Wouldn't want to be.

I am not a framer
Of the Constitution
Not a Merovingian King
Nor Charlemagne, annointed by caprice.

Am not a child of any czar
I don't think.
.

I am not the corpse
Buried beneath snow
Waiting for Spring to be found.

I am not Richard Nixon,
Neither a flaming monk of Buddha.

I am not the sum of impositions, nor subdued
By destiny.

But by my faith and its misgivings,
By will's abuse, misunderstanding,

Without me
The oceans sleep like glass
The snows do not avalanche, changing
Continuously the shape of the mountain.

Calm Under Fire

for Ted

We die in different directions
At the same pace we die
As the virtue of structure and grace

As a challenge to distance
We die, you and I, with our hands
Outreached, by chance, one night each
Toward the other. In a corner
In a cellar. With jars and webs,
A continent apart, we die

As submission to an unfinished heart.

Fear of Dreaming

Too many teeth
In this city
Are bared.

What I want is to sleep
inside a strange language, trimming

The bonsai under glass,
                              its redolent needles

clipped precise as The Buddha's fingernails.

Yet, I'm nervous to sleep. Afraid to dream
And fearful as well of waking too late.

Wary of the end of this century,
Its bloodthirsty and dead weight.

Poem

The people down
The hallway who
Stab each other
Each Friday night . . .

Is that a ritual

Or just something terribly unresolved?

Epiphany

Brutal the wind, a Bronze Age
Kind of evening outside

Watching the film *Angel Heart*
on TV, sitting up on the bed

During the scene
Of Angel and Epiphany
Making love in a room
Gone wrong in New Orleans

While blood flowed
from the ceiling, so forceful
It splashed off their bodies,

Covered the walls, the wicker
Chairs, the washbasin, the wicker
Table on which it lay.

Transfixed, watching this
And Winter, I move up closer,
The sound of heat arriving
Through the old, corner radiator

As that scene changes
To Dobermans snarling,

And the steam builds, I hear
Rapid drops loudly on varnished wood

It was coming through the ceiling
From the radiator, one flight up,
Its valve burst again, I suppose

And Angel is pulling
An old man's head from an enormous vat
Of gumbo in which he drowned. Drowned.
▪

I go to the corner and hold out
My hand to catch the drops, the low
Thumping of water on flesh . . . a small pool
forms in my palm, it's oxydized, iodine-colored.

It shocks me
I wipe my hand on the wall
Leave a faint print there . . . I've always feared

The color brown
For some reason
It's all coming together now

Angel was a soldier in Times Square
It's New Year's Eve. A flashback

I watch my hand-
Print dry on the white wall
It's shriveled, more like a paw

Epiphany holds her child
At the end,
Brutal tonight,

A world where
Even the synchronicities arrive
From up there, filled with rust

Inauguration Day

Television cameras vacillate from Monticello
To Earth orbit to Charlottesville, Virginia

Astronauts in thirty-million-dollar suits
to Thomas Jefferson. I have trouble trusting

Anyone who loses their voice too often.

Our new Secretary of State is a partner
In the largest entertainment law firm
In Hollywood and if you don't understand
Through personal experience the complete
and awesome ramifications of that, allow me
To assure you
They are staggering.

In space
They're walking
Out from the capsule. Inside
The capsule they are gauging the ozone
                                        Rips
in the atmosphere.
                    In the Athanor
                                    it's waking
The purer fire is diluted
                    orange-hot rivets of bad blood . . .

Strange transitions going on today

In Washington, D.C., in Charlottesville,
In Hollywood, In Orbit, in
                            Baghdad in the atmosphere
In the Athanor
And here, in my room, hearing
The music next door, I turn down
The TV sound
                    Everyone's hands in Washington raised
▪

To their hearts
Fervently, as if applying
                    Pressure
to a wound, slowly bleeding

A new president takes
An old oath on an old Bible

                    In Space

Walking.   Through my wall,

Music . . . The Who.   The TV tint

Gone all awry
              So every face a monsoon-cloud

shade of blue . . . the color

                    Of Kali, the fertile

goddess of chaos,
As she waits for this her age to end.

In Washington, all cameras
Closeup on Mr. Clinton

                    Pete's lyrics

reaching through:

              "Meet the new boss,
               Same as the old boss."

In Time, AIDS

The sun's shadows at dawn lay a splint on
The streets below, as if they were broken
Last night by the sounds and prowling cold

And daylight arrives like a paramedic, setting
The fractures by crudely snapping
Them into place once more.

One day I'll learn
You can't beat the odds dealt out in dreams
By dwarves with fever sores on their lips
Reciting weekly fates to narcoleptics
In bicycle shorts outside the Welfare office, Chelsea.

No wonder I lose my sense of time,
Wondering, worrying if friends have learned
Their lesson, downtown and west at the docks

Where the slaughter houses leave open
Their trucks' tailgates,
So the conquistadors and sedated snake
Charmers can have a small place in dead-scented darkness
To dance around the howling sombrero.

No matter that they forgo frostbite
When they're on the row in Satin and Spangled
Pumps . . . it's the price a man pays to cross
Dress in Winter. The price to wear taffeta

In snow and night, driven. To be modern
In the city is to be a victim in time,

Since that time, my brother, since that time.

Song

It goes, it
Goes
like an unsolved song, it goes

like the whispers through
a mirror, shaving
Your features distort
With a jet-stream clarity

It goes with vanquished steam-
gray desire, the last vapors
of your dreams, palm
tree monastic
Music

It goes
On sundial wheels
Sleeping fearfully with time
turning over what we owe, it goes

So silent, so slow
Like the Germanic cough-
Drop dissolving
On John Cage's cautious tongue

It goes the moment
It comes mainly
Ferocious, yet flamingo
Milk soft

Like a forest, like rain
Like a thief
Bound and gagged
sooner or later you're bound

To know
Obdurate and spinning it's done it's witnessed
It goes

Evening News

Now there are second thoughts
At the Odessa station

A high rise
                fire
lights up
The night
                sky of Mexico City

The others continue to carry on
at the gates of the embassy
                        chanting the Zulu
Demands

It could
        have been
                a black hole it could

have been a dwarf star . . .

All we know for certain
Is that it is
                1,800 light years away

These are actual
computer-enhanced photos
                        Of Venus

That crater down there
                        is called "Eve"

That gorge to the left
                        is called
                                "Tic"

Praying Mantis

Look at it
It's all blank
The face in the photograph
Too dark for features
But the praying mantis
Just so clear
Its forelegs fingering my hair
And it's there in focus on my shoulder
It teaches me my true name
It gives me this message:
Do not strike the low the chord,
Lest its vibrations awaken the halls of Maya.

It instructs me on the ways when need be to hide
It wakens the serpent inside to throb, to burn
It pulls the arrow from my ear

And it whispers, whispers, whispers a last word
What seems the last vapors of a long dream
Like Baraka wrote, like James Brown sings
Whispers, "please, please, please."

Micky

"I am not an actress anymore,"
I heard her shout last night
In Union Square, "but a real person,

And with virtue."

Dressed
In rough trade
Attire,

She seemed so tired.

Tired
Of the city
Of the magnets
In her brain

Left side and right

That keep on
Pulling her together

When she wants
To be
So far apart.

To the National Endowment for the Arts

It's a fact
that before his death
Robert Mapplethorpe
placed thirty-six custom cameras
with automatic timers set
to last up to nine years

discreetly

In various bedrooms
of your board members
of your congressmen
your senators
your cabinet
of your fantasies,
your well-kept hidden lust and impotence
your dazzling hubris and inertia

So some night there'll be a flash
you'll barely notice
you'll think it's a distant lightning
perhaps
and I suppose, in a way, it is
It is heat lightning
from his grave,
a freeze frame of your virulent hypocrisy

which exposed
loses all immunity
in its systems
its censoring bureaucracy

It's a record
to be collected
some day
soon

■

by thirty-six righteous men

Who are waiting
even now
at your door.

Coda

I have been becoming as I
Have been answering for fortune
Extended even as I have been
Losing lately, forming in perfunctory

Ways to go on giving, yet totalling
Up what I am
Owing, knowing how
Much is due

Doing now what is
Needed for what
I am becoming

About the Author

Poet, musician, and diarist Jim Carroll was born and grew up in New York City. Talented at both basketball and writing, he attended Trinity High School in Manhattan on a scholarship and was an All-City basketball star—a period in his life vividly described in his widely praised book *The Basketball Diaries*. Carroll's first collection of poetry, *Living at the Movies*, was published in 1973 when he was twenty-two. His other books include *The Book of Nods* (1986) and *Forced Entries* (1987). His works have appeared in such publications as *Rolling Stone*, *Poetry*, and *The Paris Review*; in the film *Poetry in Motion*; and on the album *Life Is a Killer*. As leader of the Jim Carroll Band, he recorded three albums for Atlantic Records, *Catholic Boy*, *Dry Dreams*, and *I Write Your Name*. *Praying Mantis*, a spoken-word recording, was released by Giant Records in 1991. *A World Without Gravity: The Best of the Jim Carroll Band* has just been released by Rhino Records. All of his books are available in Penguin editions.

A WORLD WITHOUT GRAVITY

The only Jim Carroll musical career retrospective

Features the best songs from
the Jim Carroll Band's
acclaimed studio albums,
including

"People Who Died"
"Work Not Play"
"It's Too Late"

plus
three previously unreleased tracks.

Compiled with input from Jim Carroll,
who also co-wrote the booklet notes with guitarist Lenny Kaye.

To order, call RHINO at
1-800-432-0020
7 days a week, 24 hours a day